Of Such a Nature / Índole

José Kozer

Of Such a Nature / Índole

Translated by Peter Boyle

The University of Alabama Press
Tuscaloosa

The University of Alabama Press
Tuscaloosa, Alabama 35487-0380
uapress.ua.edu

Inquiries about reproducing material from this work
should be addressed to the University of Alabama Press
Índole was first published in 2012 by
Ediciones Matanzas, Matanzas, Cuba

Typeface: Scala Pro

Cover image: *Snow Within* by Kazuaki Tanahashi;
courtesy of the artist
Cover design: Steve Miller

Cataloging-in-Publication data is available from the Library of Congress.
ISBN: 978-0-8173-5905-8
E-ISBN: 978-08173-9167-6

Contents

Acknowledgments

Índole was originally published in Spanish by Ediciones Matanzas, Cuba, in 2012.

I wish to thank the editors of the following magazines where several of these translations first appeared, sometimes in an earlier version: *Cordite, Rabbit, Review: Literature and arts of the Americas,* and *Statement.*

José Kozer

I would like to acknowledge gratefully the assistance of José Kozer, who helped with the clarification of difficult and unusual words and phrases and patiently explained a range of local references and Cubanisms. His willingness to answer my various questions and point out various confusions on my part has been invaluable. My thanks are also due to Chris Andrews, who carefully read through various drafts of these translations and added his suggestions. The final responsibility for these translations, with whatever errors they may contain, is my own.

My translations have also been informed by the interviews, commentaries, and scholarly articles gathered in Jacobo Sefamí's *La voracidad grafómana: José Kozer,* and by the lengthy interview with Kozer by Sefamí in *De la imaginación poética.* I also wish to thank all those who have made readings by Kozer available to the general public over the web. The opportunity to hear him perform his poetry has been of great value in my efforts to grasp his approach to poetry as well as the content of his work.

Peter Boyle

Introduction
Peter Boyle

José Kozer (Havana, 1940) is one of Latin America's most distinguished, and most prolific, poets. He is the author of over ninety books, including *Este judío de números y letras* (1975), *Bajo este cien* (1983), *La garza sin sombras* (1985), *Carece de causa* (1988), and *Y del esparto la invariabilidad* (2005). His books have been published in Mexico, Spain, Argentina, Brazil, Cuba, and Venezuela, as well as in bilingual editions in the United States and England. In 2013, he was awarded the highly prestigious Pablo Neruda Prize in Chile (the major prize for poetry in the Spanish-speaking world).[1] This was an especially significant event, not only because it marks his recognition as an enduring poet whose work will last into the future, but also because the award comes to him despite the many difficulties of classification and acceptance that his poetry has encountered.

Living in the United States since 1960 (apart from a few years in Spain), Kozer discovered himself as a Cuban poet inside the United States, mostly having to relearn Spanish in his late twenties and early thirties in order to be a poet in Spanish, realizing that only in the language of his childhood and adolescence would poetry be possible for him. While many of his poems have a clear Cuban setting that reflects his childhood and his family home in Havana, many more have a location that is hard to identify: an apartment, a house in a wintry climate, a room, a garden with various (tropical or Northeast American) birds, perhaps a monastery in Japan, or somewhere on the steppes of Russia. When I was translating his book *Anima,* I had assumed from several poems that Kozer visited Japan, specifically Mount Yoshino, and stayed there to learn Zen, but these locations came into his poems from his reading, from his translations (out of English) of poetry by Japanese poet-monks, and from an intensely vivid imagination. Kozer's poetry challenges a certain, often unconscious, tendency to read poems as a form of autobiography and to value or dismiss a poet in terms of their life, their story, or the sociological content of their poems rather than the poetry itself.

Kozer's poems resist classification. They are not (for the most part) primarily poems of exile, of migrant experience, even in the sense of family life or Jewish identity, or poems descriptive of nature, though all those topics can be found in his work. There is a strong ethical drive in Kozer's poetry, a profound sense of continuity with his Jewish ancestry, and a powerful element of Buddhist practice as the poem becomes an act of complete immersion in the present, but these driving forces are contained within an aesthetic that demands absolute freedom for the poem. In his essay "The Argentine Writer and Tradition" Jorge Borges argues that writers from the margin, rather than accepting the role of supplying "local color" to the metropolis, should see themselves as the inheritors of European literature, free in a unique way to play with all of it (426). In the twenty-first century "world literature" would be more to the point than Borges's narrower "European literature." Kozer's poetry inhabits that unique freedom as a matter of course.

To get a clearer picture of what Kozer's poems are about and how best to approach them it is necessary to take a step back and look more closely at his biography (including his early development as a writer) and at the general state of Latin American poetry in the 1970s and 1980s.

José Kozer: From Childhood in Havana to Poet in New York

Born in Havana in 1940, José Kozer was the son of Jewish immigrants, David Kozer and Ana Katz. His father arrived in Havana from Poland in 1927 hoping to enter the United States, but ended up staying in Cuba. A Polish Jew fluent in Polish and Yiddish, he never mastered Spanish, remaining unable to read or write the language and speaking it only falteringly with a strong Yiddish accent. He had been a Marxist and a Communist but became disillusioned with all political utopias after the betrayal of those ideals by Stalin. Though always proudly Jewish, he rejected traditional orthodoxy and favored assimilation. His talk was often of communism, Trotsky, Lenin, and the heroes of pre-Stalinist Marxism. José's mother, Ana, was the daughter of Isaac Katz who had come to Cuba from Czechoslovakia in 1924 and brought his wife, a son, and three daughters there in 1929. Working hard to support himself and his family in their new country, Isaac Katz established the grocery store La Bodega Cubana in downtown Havana. He was deeply religious, a traditional orthodox Jew and a founder of Adath Israel, the first Ashkenazi synagogue in Cuba. José's mother observed the outward forms of religion but was more concerned with appearances. Her mother, José's grandmother, Elena Katz, was even more devoutly religious than her husband. Though never literate in Spanish, Isaac Katz made sure that his children would all speak and write perfect Spanish, and so José's mother was fluent in the language and spoke it with a flawless Cuban accent. Kozer grew up, then, in a very complex family with a multitude of strong, conflicting presences.

One of the first battles between his parents was over where José should be educated. His mother favored a traditional Jewish school, but his father insisted on a secular school where his son would grow up among Cubans as a Cuban. His father won. Kozer once summarized the result of that decision in these words:

> Aquí entra la nueva generación, la asimilada: yo soy cubano (Sólo mucho más tarde descubriría, aceptaría que lo soy sin dejar de ser lo otro, el otro: judío del otro lado del Jordán).[2]

> Here the new generation comes in, the assimilated one: I am Cuban (Only much later would I discover, would I accept that I'm Cuban without ceasing to be other, the other: a Jew from the other side of the Jordan).

From age five to fifteen, the family lived in Estrada Palma 515, between Goicuría and Juan Delgado, in the Santos Suárez neighborhood of Havana. His father was a tailor and door-to-door clothing salesman who came to Cuba from Germany alone. All of his family—his parents and brothers—perished in the Holocaust either in the Warsaw ghetto or in Nazi concentration camps with one exception: an uncle whom José met much later in a poor neighborhood of Tel Aviv, who was already dying and in the grip of Alzheimer's. José's father was largely silent around the house, tongue-tied in Spanish, and at odds with his wife's conventional middle-class view of religion; he had lost his youthful revolutionary ideals having so much to express but no way to say it. Other powerful presences in José's childhood were his grandfather Isaac Katz, with his profound goodness and generosity, and his grandmother. "Grandmother is in slippers, wandering though the house like a ghost . . . She smells of kitchens, of coal. Grandmother is a smell. She smells of Old Havana."[3]

This world of the family home in Havana recurs frequently within Kozer's poetry. One function of his writing is to hold together his double heritage as Cuban and Jewish. Another function is to give voice to his father and his Grandfather Katz, both of whom could write only a limited

Spanish with much difficulty. Through experimentation, word play, and the accumulation of semantic layers, Kozer's poetry also embodies (not sentimentally but with unflinching honesty) the Biblical injunction "Honor thy father and thy mother." It is one (by no means the only one) of the trajectories marked by his poetry. As Kozer writes, he stays inside the room of his poetry "to resist death, madness, [and] the cataclysms of history" knowing that poetry binds together and provides continuity.[4]

As a teenager José Kozer read voraciously: Defoe and Rousseau; the great nineteenth-century novelists of Russia, France and England; Shakespeare, Dante, Melville, Cervantes; the poets of the Spanish Siglo de Oro; Conrad, Whitman, Poe, and many more, all in Spanish. He wrote a lot too, but not poetry. He imagined himself becoming a novelist, yet his writing was more like prose poetry or sketches. At seventeen, not long after starting college, he had wanted to go to the Sierra Maestra and join the revolutionaries—at which point his father promptly sent him to New York to continue his studies. Sixteen months later, in May 1959, he returned to Havana when the revolution had already broken out, but he quickly became disillusioned. Most of all, he began to realize that he was not a political type at heart. In the new Cuba being constructed there was no space for anything but politics. He made the decision to leave. His father gave him a ticket to Miami, a good suit, and a gold watch to sell, but this was all he could do to help. José flew to Miami, swapped his watch for a bus ticket to New York, and began life on his own. From 1960 to 1965, he worked first in a small business, then in the NYU Science Library. Once he graduated from New York University, he became a part-time lecturer at Queens College. He stayed at Queens College until his retirement as professor of Hispanic studies in 1997.

The years from 1960 to 1968 were especially hard for Kozer. He was alone in New York, starting a new life from scratch. His studies and paid work were all in English. Kozer felt inwardly paralyzed, unable to write, rapidly losing his language. His marriage to a North American woman proved disastrous, leading to divorce and custody disputes over their daughter. At the same time, in 1968 he got to know Isaac Goldemberg with whom he talked in Spanish constantly, gradually regaining his fluency. He also began drinking heavily, which had the effect of loosening him up, making writing possible again. It was not particularly good poetry, Kozer says, but it brought back his language and soon writing itself became a salvation. In 1972, he began spending summers in Spain. During his time in Spain, he met Guadalupe who soon became his wife and lifelong companion. His first book *Padres y otros profesiones*, published in New York in 1972, is confessional poetry, quite direct and transparent, energetic in its own way but quite unlike the poetry Kozer went on to write. By the time of *Este judío de números y letras* (1975), *Y así tomaron posesión en las ciudades* (1979), and *Jarrón de las abreviaturas* (1980), Kozer developed his own style of open poetry using distinctive paragraph-length stanzas with long lines disrupted by parentheses and rapid changes of direction, a multi-layered difficult poetry. By his mid-thirties, he had realized his adolescent dream of becoming a writer—but as a poet, not a novelist.

Post-Boom Latin American Poetry and the Neobaroque

For any Latin American wanting to be a poet in the early 1970s the weight of the past generation was overwhelming. Pablo Neruda, most of all, was the towering figure in a range of poetic genres from love poem to protest poem, from lyric to epic. There was also the more cerebral work of Octavio Paz, the ironic style of Nicanor Parra's anti-poems, the more direct conversational approach of highly engaged political poets like Ernesto Cardenal and Roque Dalton. Beside these trends lay the background, dominant position of a mostly plain-speaking, transparent style, sparse in adjectives and ornamentation, trusting in the power of sentiment to reach its audience. Antonio Machado, Miguel Hernández, and the later work of Luis Cernuda could be taken as examples of what such poetry might be like at its best, capable in the right hands (and at the right moments) of producing powerful, extraordinary work but in danger of descending into sentimentality and excessive baldness. Without wishing to dismiss their poems as merely sentimental, it might be fair to characterize the poetry of José Emilio Pacheco, Juan Gelman, Mario Benedetti, Eugenio Montejo, Álvaro Mutis, Eliseo Diego, and Gastón Baquero (to name only a few prominent poets) as fitting within that lineage. It may seem strange to include Gelman and Benedetti in the same list as Mutis, Diego, and Baquero. Gelman and Benedetti, after all, sought to communicate with the masses for political purposes and chose a simple plain style for that purpose. Such a project was never part of the aim of the other three (or of Pacheco or Montejo). However, stylistically and in terms of many underlying assumptions about how poetry should work, there is a strong affinity between the two groups. Both groups work from the belief that poetry, at its best, aspires to simplicity and talks directly to the reader with no need for rare words or syntactic convolution. There is also a degree of convergence between this dominant style and the conversational poem as it reached Latin America from the beat generation of the United States. In both cases there is a reliance on plain direct simplicity, a concern with reaching an audience, a tendency to give primacy to content and message over the aleatory, experimental, disruptive or chaotic impulses that very often generate the best poetry. Of course Latin American poetry, and Spanish poetry in general, has always contained many streams. One could also point equally to the array of experimental, surreal, densely written poetry that includes such major works as Federico García Lorca's *Poeta en Nueva York*, César Vallejo's *Trilce*, and Vincente Huidobro's *Altazor*.

A final comment worth making about this lineage of the plain, direct, transparent, closed poem concerns its impact on the reception that neobaroque poetry would have, especially perhaps poetry like Kozer's. The new wave of the neobaroque risked offending two groups of poets (as well as critics, organizers, and others on the borders of poetry). It risked antagonizing those who wanted a simplified, unambiguous poetry that could be used as a tool of mass radicalization. On the other hand, it also risked offending more traditional poets and readers of poetry (regardless of their politics) who looked to figures like Machado and Cernuda (or Montejo, Mutis, and Pacheco) as exempla of poetry at its best.[5] To take only one example, the proliferation of detail, the inclusion of banal material, the very "prosaicness" in, say, Kozer's poetry posed a problem to many in a way that such characteristics would not in a North American (or British, Irish or Australian) context. For many readers (and writers) of poetry within the Latin American world, being "anecdotal" is seen as a serious flaw, whereas grounding a poem in lived realities named specifically and described in detail is generally looked at favorably within the Anglo-Saxon world. Conversely there are some within the Anglo-Saxon world for whom the mere sight of words like "love," "pain," "sorrow," or "moon" is enough to condemn a poem out of hand as worthless.[6] The power of such deep-seated preferences also extends to the use of vulgar expressions, slang, or the deliberate breaking of grammar conventions, as well as the failure to deliver a clear, paraphrasable message. One implication of these preferences is that when the neobaroque poets first appeared their work was, for many, an unsettling rupture.

During the 1970s to 1990s, a movement began to counter what I have called the dominant position: a desire to push back the preeminence of content and audience, to give priority to what we don't know when we enter the process of writing a poem rather than what we do know, to create a complex, multi-layered, open poetry rather than a linear, more obvious, one-dimensional poetry. Neobaroque is a very loose label that has been coined to cover many of these poets. In his introduction to the influential anthology *Medusario* (1996), Uruguayan poet and critic Roberto Echavarren sees the neobaroque as a reaction against both the older avant-garde associated with Huidobro, Paz, Girondo, and the Brazilian concretists, and as a reaction against the more or less politically engaged colloquialism of Cardenal and Dalton, in favor of an "impure" poetry, "now colloquial, now opaque, now meta-poetic" rejecting any notion of "a 'via media' of poetic communication" (13–14).

> Los poetas neobarrocos . . . pasan de un nivel de referencia a otro, sin limitarse a una estrategia específica, o a cierto vocabulario, o a una distancia irónica fija. Puede decirse que no tienen estilo, ya que más bien se deslizan de un estilo a otro sin volverse los prisioneros de una posición o procedimiento. (14)

> The neobaroque poets . . . move from one reference level to another without limiting themselves to a [single] specific strategy or certain vocabulary or a fixed ironic distance. You could say they have no style, or more exactly that they slide from one style to another without becoming prisoners of a [single] position or way of proceeding.

Medusario, as a "muestra" ("demonstration," "showcasing") of a new style of Latin American poetry, includes (among many others) the Mexican poets Gerardo Deniz, David Huerta, and Coral Bracho; the Peruvian Rodolfo Hinostroza; the Uruguayan poets Marosa di Giorgio, Eduardo Milán, Eduardo Espina, and Roberto Echavarren; the Brazilian poets Haroldo de Campos, Wilson Bueno, and Paulo Leminski; and the Argentine poets Reynaldo Jiménez,[7] Osvaldo Lamborghini, and Néstor Perlongher. The extreme diversity of this anthology, ranging from the intensely personal, borderline surreal prose poetry of Marosa di Giorgio to the more abstract language games of Reynaldo Jiménez, underscores Echavarren's point that the neobaroque does not consist of any one style. There is also the significant difference between the humorous, ironic poetry of Deniz and the visceral, politically engaged work of Chilean poet Raúl Zurita whose poetry is also included in *Medusario*.[8] José Kozer is one of the editors of this anthology as well as being represented in it, placing his poetic work within this very loose grouping.

Before being grouped together under the label neobaroque, each of these poets found their own way towards a more richly textured, complicated, open style of poetry in more or less conscious opposition to the transparent, content-and-audience-focused poetry of what Echavarren terms "los coloquialistas." In Kozer's case, the transition away from his earliest poetry in *Padres y otros profesiones* (1972) towards his denser poems of the mid-eighties, found in books like *Bajo este cien* (1983) and *La garza sin sombras* (1985), was in many ways influenced by his reading North American poets like Ezra Pound, William Carlos Williams, Charles Olson, and Wallace Stevens. This interaction between North American and Latin American literature is nothing new. One has only to think of the impact of Whitman on Latin American poetry, or, in the opposite direction, the impact of César Vallejo on James Wright. Very rapidly, Kozer developed a style that is highly distinctive and, in important ways, unlike any North American model. To make sense of that style—Kozer's very specific manner of being neobaroque—it is necessary to consider both the more visible, outward aspects of his style and the underlying energy, the driving forces of his poetry.

Aesthetic Preferences, a Buddhist Practice and the Weight of the Command "Write This Down": The Poetics of a Kozer Poem

There is great diversity in the content and the emotional "feel" of Kozer's poems, but also a remarkable consistency in their layout and poetic strategies. Kozer's Jewish heritage is announced in the very title of his first book that he considered significant, *Este judío de números y letras* (1975).

Buddhist and East Asian themes can be seen as early as "Zen" published in *Jarrón de las abreviaturas* (1980) or "El filósofo Mo Tse enseña" published in *Y así tomaron posesión en las ciudades* (1979). Poems of love for Guadalupe, of everyday life, of reflection on mystics and writers, and of his childhood in Cuba can all be seen from *La garza sin sombras* (1985) onwards, if not earlier. Where some poets might have developed different stylistic approaches for such diverse materials, Kozer employs a consistent, though progressively more elaborate, style for each topic or purpose.

The distinctive elements of a Kozer poem include a layout with the paragraph as the fundamental unit, the use of run-on lines that both speed up and interrupt the poem's flow, frequent changes in direction through the disruption of sentence structure, the omission of most punctuation, and the use of parentheses to shift focus as the reader makes their way through a poem that constantly twists and turns as it progresses. In addition, one could point to an extensive, often unusual, vocabulary that includes Cubanisms and local words from many parts of the Spanish-speaking world alongside archaic formal words. There is a preference for the precise term over the generic word—"majagua" (blue mahoe) rather than "madera" (wood), "corneja" (crow) rather than "pájaro" (bird)—for local or scientific names of plants and animals over the more traditional poetic vocabulary.

Kozer's poems typically proceed through elaboration, ambiguity, and abrupt shifts in tone and language level. Yet the primary purpose of these strategies is not to shift attention to language itself, away from what is being expressed, nor is Kozer's focus (in the vast majority of his poems) the failure of language to capture experiences or a desire to rest in contemplation of the strangeness of language, either as spoken medium or as configuration of signs on a page. In an extensive interview with Jacobo Sefamí, Kozer states that calling his poetry neobaroque or concerned with language is only one way to situate it, but that calling it religious might be even more valid.

> Yo no tengo un problema de lenguaje, tengo un problema religioso, metafísico, filosófico, ético. El language después de todo no es un en sí, es un instrumento; no es una autonomía, es un vehículo . . . a mí sí me conmueve la dificultad religiosa, la dificultad ante la muerte del cuerpo. (319–20)

I don't have a problem of language, I have a religious, metaphysical, philosophical, ethical problem. Language after all is not an end in itself, it's an instrument; it's not autonomous, it's a vehicle . . . yes, for me, what moves me is religious difficulty, the difficulty before the death of the body.

These comments are an important reminder that the difficulties in Kozer's poetry are not there as an end in themselves but rather as strategies for intensification, for reaching more deeply into what the poem might reveal.

In an important essay on Kozer's poetics, Eduardo Espina analyzes the various structural devices typical of Kozer's poetry, highlighting the way the aural dimension of his poetry works in combination with its visual presence (Espina, 285–304). The layout and sound of the poem go together, making Kozer's poetry quite different from free verse with its widely varying line lengths, let alone the prose poem. The language itself is often densely "prosaic," highly specific, containing abrupt, very colloquial expressions alongside scientific or archaic words, but the rhythm accentuated by repetitions and alliteration (especially when delivered in a reading by Kozer) marks a strong, almost traditional, sense of poetry as performance. In Espina's words, Kozer's poetry "devuelve a la página la musicalidad de los primeros días de la palabra" [returns to the page the musicality of the first days of poetry] (291). The versicle layout in the form

xxxxxxxxxxxxxxxxxxxxxxxxxxxxxxxxxxxx
    xxxxxxxx
    xxxxxxxx
    xxxxxxxx
    xxxxxxxx

marks a distance from prose, both encouraging, and in places interrupting, the forward flow of the poem. It can also be seen as a visual sign both of a biblical scroll that the *yad* or pointer moves down, and of a Chinese or Japanese scroll where poetry is a visual, as well as auditory, aesthetic experience. This way of reading the layout is further suggested by the general absence of punctuation, the sudden shifts in grammatical structure, the tendency for past tense to glide into present tense, and for the third person pronouns or verb endings to suddenly become first person: in short, a multitude of devices that help create an experience of simultaneity and immediacy rather than the passive recounting of one's own story purely as story. There is, then, a complex relationship between the *what* of Kozer's poetry and its form both as sound and as visual object. The use of parentheses, as much a signature device of Kozer's as the versicle form, signals the need to include, complicate, and adhere to the difficulty and multiplicity of experience. The reader (and the poet himself in the act of creating) is alerted to slow down, to remain attentive and not let the sweep of sound substitute itself for the difficult task of being in the present.

If Kozer has remained for so many years with one stylistic form across so many poems of significantly diverse content, then it may be that the form operates as a tie, a bind, a ligament to two different, but in important respects complementary, traditions. There is the weight of his Jewish heritage, both its mysticism and the specific task of carrying the stories of his silent (and silenced) father and grandfather. The blurring of time implicit in the form becomes, in a poem like "Indicios, del inscrito" from *Carece de causa* (1988), a mode of registering the way the time of King David and the prophets Elijah and Isaiah collapses into the time of the death of Kozer's grandfather, Isaac Katz, on May 20, 1956 in Havana (or, perhaps better expressed, the way grandfather's death enters into the time, the reality, of those Kings and prophets).

A second trajectory that is marked by Kozer's form is the Buddhist vision of being in the present and the illusory nature of all attachments, including the attachment to our own specific story and the tendency as writers and poets to say (at least implicitly) "This is important because it happened to *me*." Buddhism insists on the illusory nature of that *me*, of the autobiographic cry. It could be argued that the form of Kozer's poems, the deliberate aesthetic choice of dislocation, disruption, and the collapse of linearity, work in large measure to undermine the expectations of narrative. This helps explain why, for all their accumulation of detail, Kozer's poems feel so different from autobiographic (or biographic) poems by such North American poets as Robert Lowell, Philip Levine, Robert Hass, Galway Kinnell or Charles Wright. There is none of the closure one finds in the form of a poetically sharpened story. Instead, Kozer opts to undercut narrative, leaving us with either stillness or the perpetually off-center. At the same time, Kozer's aesthetic is not that of language poetry. Zen, Jewish mysticism, the immediate, the body as our corporeal reality, death as our imminent future: these topoi might be considered the focus of Kozer's poetry, not language or the nature of representation.

One final significant aspect of Kozer's poetics is his manner of writing itself. For the past forty years or more Kozer has written a poem every day in the early morning, writing intensely with absolute focus for twenty or thirty minutes. He picks a specific space, at one time the basement in his house in Forest Hills, later a room in his apartment in Hallandale, to practice this morning ritual. Later, the poems are lightly edited if necessary, typed up and placed in folders, *carpetas*, organized by date. When Jacobo Sefamí interviewed Kozer in May 1990 there were already 2,800 poems. By the time Sefamí prepared the 2013 edition of *De la imaginación poética* there were already more than 9,000 (Sefamí, 251–52) and as of December 12, 2016, there were 11,518.[9] Of this vast storehouse of Kozer's poems (some of them quite long) only a small fraction has been published. This gulf between the production of poetry and its likelihood of publication suggests that the writing of poetry is, for Kozer, a contemplative practice. Publication, let alone fame or a mass audience, if it is a consideration at all, is secondary. One could argue that Kozer approaches the ideal of an almost impersonal simplicity central to a poet like Antonio Machado, but does so through an array of poetic procedures opposite to Machado. For all their complexity the poems carry that feel of Zen immediacy, of approaching stillness that locates Kozer's poetry as closer, after all, to the contemplative Machado than to the Anglo-Saxon tradition of the highly detailed autobiographic poem.

Índole

Índole. (Del lat. indoles). 1. f. Condición e inclinación natural propia de cada persona. 2. f. Naturaleza, calidad y condición de las cosas.[10]

Índole (From Latin indoles) 1. Natural condition and inclination specific to an individual. 2. The nature, quality and condition of things.

The word "índole" might be used in the Spanish for all these expressions: "a type," "a kind," "a sort," "things like that," "people of that ilk," "that sort of thing," "he was a hot-headed type," or "this is a very tricky type of question." "*Índole*" suggests, then, that the poems gathered in this collection, published in Matanzas, Cuba in 2012, are all exempla or instances of specific types of situations, things, or experiences. Nearly every poem has a title beginning "*Véase como . . .*" or simply "*Véase . . .,*" literally "Let it be seen," and translating approximately to "See how," though with a more formal feel. That formality adds to the humor in titles like "Véase si todo lo que se dice a continuación aclara algo" ("Wherein it is seen whether all that's said later clarifies anything") or "Véase, hasta para un chino, la imposibilidad de alcanzar la escritura" ("Wherein it's seen how, even for someone Chinese, it's impossible to understand writing"), alerting the reader to the shifting ironic glance that so often holds together the most mundane, rarely spoken-of aspects of life, and a range of more serious concerns. I have chosen to emphasize that formality by translating the phrase as "Wherein it is seen," highlighting the implication that the poems form a series of sometimes ironic, sometimes more serious, exempla. Kozer's poetry collections tend to be organized around specific recurrent titles: in *Anima* (2002) almost all the poems are titled "Anima," in *Acta* (2010) most poems are titled "Acta." Even where the titles of individual poems vary, the collections tend to be organized around a dominant subject matter. Thus *Carece de causa* (1988) gathers poems about Kozer's Jewish heritage and *Tokonoma* (2011) consists of poems with Chinese or Japanese Buddhist content. We could, then, perhaps describe *Índole* as a gathering of poems of everyday life.

At least from the time of the lake poets in England in the late eighteenth century the desire to bring poetry back to everyday reality, to the life lived by everybody rather than high-flown poeticism, has been a recurrent project. Whether it is Baudelaire writing of the crowded poverty of nineteenth-century Paris or Frank O'Hara's *Lunch Poems*, Machado's return to Soria or Neruda's *Odas elementales*, this return to the everyday is announced repeatedly in Western poetry. Even in this very short list the staggering diversity of what people might mean by "everyday life" or "everyday reality" is clear. In the case of Kozer's poetry, it is above all the reality of the body, of daily rituals like cleansing, cooking, eating and the enormous task (in all its guises) of waiting. The sense of life stripped bare, brought back to its minima, comes through in so many Kozer poems. There is frequently the presence of his wife Guadalupe, the memory of his father, and references to his favorite poets and composers—Mandelstam, Akhmatova, and Gorecki among others—yet the dominant mood is of solitude, of life approaching its minimum. This focus on corporeal rituals is less a product of the realities of his specific life than a question of aesthetic choices. Beyond the accidents of biography, the variations in what might be meant by "everyday life" reflect what a poet chooses to include within their poetry in order to create a particular approach to reality. One could, for example, contrast "everyday life" as represented by Frank O'Hara with José Kozer's poetry on the topic. It is not that Kozer has never had dinner with friends and walked the streets of New York, or that O'Hara never showered or cleaned his teeth. It is, rather, a matter of aesthetic choices based on one's vision of reality, the specific dimension of life, and (for O'Hara perhaps especially) the projection of the self that a poet chooses to explore.

For Kozer, it is most often about locating oneself, locating the speaker of the poem, within the presence of death, both one's own death and the deaths of parents and ancestors. However a poem in *Índole* may start, it frequently ends up contemplating the body's decline into old age and the imminence of death. These potentially overwhelmingly dark images are softened, varied, held in check by persistent humor, a zany inventiveness in language, and the leaps made between disparate things. Part of the fun of these poems (and the challenge to the poet) lies in seeing how the most improbable material may be incorporated into poetry, may act as a trigger for serious reflections. Cleaning one's dentures in the morning, eating or trying to eat a brown rice cake, a woman leaning over a bowl of oatmeal, a salamander glimpsed while eating breakfast: such small events are a sample of the opening gambits of these poems that may lead in any number of directions.

The first poem of the book "Véase como a fin de cuentas acaba en empate " ("Wherein it is seen how, when all is said and done, it comes out a draw") opens with the rejection of Romantic universals, Shelley's Universal Mind, and insists on the mind's singularities, which in turn rapidly become the body's singularities—loss of appetite, diarrhea, and growing mental confusion. A confession of ignorance moves the poem forward crab-like with a doubled-over image of time passing: sand falling in a clepsydra. The Socratic declaration "I don't know anything" is delivered in a humorous ironic tone. The poem closes with the shared contemplation between the speaker and a caterpillar of minimal food: a mulberry leaf and some brown bread. It is a poem returning us to an earth of simplicity, our corporeal failing selves.

The poem "Véase como el oficial de marina no nos revela su vida secreta" ("Wherein it is seen how the navy officer does not reveal his secret life to us") explores the theme of a journey to the end of life through references to Conrad, the Bible, and Buddhist traditions. The navy officer on retirement sets off on a river "navigable in all its length as / far as the end of the world, / as Judgment Day," leaving behind his mountain of books, including his first edition Conrad, sailing alone toward Judgment Day to fish. Poetry takes on the role here of a preparation for death. In the next poem in the collection "Véase como siempre acaba en lo mismo" ("Wherein it is seen how it always ends up the same") the Buddhist practice of meditation as preparation for death is approached with Beckett-like humor as the narrator attempts, with numerous asides, to concentrate only on his breath and banish all thoughts. In the process, he imagines becoming a statue of Saint Francis, complete with birds perching on him, then he succumbs to angry thoughts about his father, only to conclude imagining the washerwomen of the Caspian sea and the secret knowledge of their fragrance shared by father and son.

If Beckett is one valid point of comparison for the poems in Índole, the immense, endlessly extrapolating, self-exploratory and open-ended work of Michel de Mointaigne would be another. Just as Montaigne's essays, or assays of the self and of the state of his thoughts, are a collection of often deliberately eccentric pieces all beginning "On . . ." or "Of . . .," so Kozer's assemblage of poems titled "Véase . . ." could be seen as a series of attempts, or essays (assays), to answer an unstated central question: "What is it to be human?" As in Montaigne's essays, Kozer's poems frequently convey the sense of writing as preparation for death and, also like Montaigne, Kozer revels in the ability to start in one place and end up somewhere quite different. Montaigne's essay "On Coaches" is a good example of this procedure.[11] Both Kozer and Montaigne frequently use references to a range of authors to extend their thinking and complicate the texture and ethical stance of their work. Thus, among the poems in Índole there are references to Shelley, Conrad, Mandelstam, Akhmatova, Marina Tsvestayeva, Saint Therese, and Yang Wan Li, among others. There are also echoes of different styles creating implicit references to poets. For example, in "Véase como a fin de cuentas acaba en empate" ("Wherein it is seen how, when all's said and done, it comes out a draw") the phrase "Ah la muerte, leda / Muerte" recalls Renaissance poetry with the archaic word "leda" (gentle, happy, mild). In the English version, I have echoed the rather Shakespearean (at this moment) Keats for the same effect: "Ah death, easeful / Death." The Buddhist sutras and the Bible, as well as Kafka, Pound, and perhaps Ovid, are also incorporated into the poetry in this way.

The tendency of Kozer's poems in *Índole* is to spiral outwards, moving rapidly by association from point to point. In "Véase, como dice Eduardo Espina, que todo es mental" ("Where it is seen how, as Eduardo Espina says, 'it's all in the mind'"), the poem opens with the declaration "Gradually I'm stretching out dawn." This humorous claim to omnipotence is followed by a description of the speaker cleaning his dentures, an activity which becomes for him "the most inward dwelling place," comparable to a reverie of Saint Theresa of Avila. Next, a fantasy of watching fresh bread come out of an oven morphs into a description of the entire process of the creation of bread starting with the wheat being planted. All this is shared with an imaginary "Petronila," a common maid's name in prerevolutionary Cuba, who soon becomes the guide of a desert caravan, leading to further confusions of time and place. In the end, the poet draws the line with the assertion that going any further would be "a bad mental habit." Irony and humor dominate this poem in its play with the Zen concept of being fully present in each instant, finding one's "inward dwelling place" neither in the past nor the future but in a now that turns out to be as problematic as anything else.

Kozer's poetry of the everyday can be seen as a sometimes humorous, at times disturbing, evocation of the shared bedrock of existence. In *Everyday Life: Theories and Practices from Surrealism to the Present*, Michael Sheringham argues that "to focus on the everyday is to pull back from the perceived world just enough to be able to see generically—patterns, rhythms, repetitions—but not so far as to analyse, delimit or pigeon-hole" (128). To write of the everyday is, then, a very serious task since the quotidian, the banal, the overlooked, the ordinary is precisely "ce que nous sommes" ("what we are") (Sheringham, 249). Bypassing poeticisms and the abstractions of traditional philosophy, to approach the everyday is to challenge unexamined hierarchies and to look for what might connect us to our depths.

One other important side of the everyday presented in several poems in *Índole,* as across the wider range of Kozer's poetry, is his love for his wife Guadalupe and the daily routines of their shared life. "Véase como se alcanza la felicidad con un poco de imaginación" ("Wherein it is seen how happiness is achieved with a little imagination") opens with the image of two lovers naked eating fish cakes. While their unusual attire and the way they stroll together as lovers provide "some / distraction for the / neighborhood," there is also a serious point being made: that keeping one's desires simple can offer the best chance for happiness. Yet this poem, as so often in Kozer, twists again at the end. After their walk, the couple strip naked, but not for lovemaking as the reader might imagine, rather "to wait for the / cranky bitchy Bitch" who never turns up as a couple, in other words to wait for death, the unpredictable, nearly always singular, final visitor. "Dos índoles, una devastación" ("Two índoles, a devastation") compares José's love for Guadalupe with Propertius's love for Cynthia. Humor dominates in this poem that implicitly references Pound as much as Propertius, but also contrasts the pose of obsessive romantic love with a lifelong, companionable, domestic love: "We / coped / (will / cope: / you've / got / to / trust)." The poem closes not with any image of death this time, but with the presence of Guadalupe, "a / live / coal / still."

The last two poems in *Índole* shift their focus to Cuba's poverty, the life of poverty faced by most Cubans before and after the revolution. The state of exile, the various waves of exile, is alluded to in the lines from "Acta": "The caiman has gone, those left have gone, / we've all gone." There is a strong sense of the grief of exile as those gone can be recognized by a "twist of corn stalk / knotted into the / buttonhole of a / jacket." As Leymen Pérez notes in a review of *Índole,* Kozer's homeland is sharply present in the language of this poem with its accumulation of Indo-Antillean words "guásimas," "caiman," "guano," "yarey," "bibijagua," "bijirita," and "cocuyo."[12] Kozer's "plurilingüístico vocabulario" (multilinguistic vocabulary), in Pérez's phrase, presents a problem to the translator. A "bibijagua" is a leafcutter ant and a "bijirita" is a flame-throated warbler, but the original words inscribe themselves as quintessentially Cuban in a way that disappears in translation. Cuba is inscribed through word choice throughout the poem, something gently foreshadowed in the opening with its play on the word for a hardware store: "ferreterías" (standard Spanish) against "tlapalerías" (Mexican Spanish). Nostalgia for Cuba, though, is only one aspect of this poem. In my reading, "Acta" goes beyond the sadness of exile to look towards a future where Cubans in exile and at home sit down together "as a family" in their easy chairs and "start to tell stories," to solve their future together without external pressure. It is, then, not just a poem of grief or nostalgia but a poem of hope.

If in "Acta" hope is one element that serves to balance nostalgia, throughout *Índole*, as across the body of Kozer's poetry in general, two forces, it seems to me, modify an often bleak (though entirely realistic) view of the human condition. First, the sheer energy of Kozer as inventor, taker of leaps, flouter of conventions, does much to modify what might otherwise be an overwhelming gloom. In "Devastación" ("Devastation"), for example, when contemplating the horrors of the twentieth century, the speaker portrays himself after death as dancing "arm in arm" with Mandelstam, Gumilyov, Bely, Blok, and Akhmatova, "farting in Stalin's / face so he can smell / his own dead." Poetry, then, is an energy that fights back and ultimately has the last word over pharaohs, tsars, and other twentieth-century despots. Even if "at the heights" there is "no sign of God" in this world, the rebellious energy of poetry is a kind of hope. The second force that works against bleakness is what I would call the Buddhist side of Kozer. Many of his poems exemplify a form of attention that, in certain moments, brings multiple times together and, in a sense, abolishes time. Two poems from earlier collections that illustrate this process very powerfully are "Encuentro en Cho-Fu-Sa" ("A meeting at Cho-Fu-Sa") (*Stet* 2006, 56-61) and "Ánima por George Oppen" ("Anima for George Oppen") (*Anima* 2011, 254–57). The first is a masterful reworking of Li Po and Pound where the young Chinese woman waiting for her merchant husband transforms into the speaker's wife Guadalupe flying in to Fort Lauderdale to reunite with the poet. In the second poem, while on a train to Munich, approaching the rail link to Dachau, the speaker reads a poem by Oppen based on a poem by Buddhadeva Bose and prepares to eat an apple when, in one vision, Japanese and German landscapes, Cézanne's painting of an apple, Buddhism, Kant on his deathbed, and the dead of the Holocaust fuse in a moment of simultaneity. Traces of such mysticism, combining Buddhist and Jewish Kabbalistic roots, illuminate José Kozer's poetry, giving it its unique depth of feeling and insight.

Notes

1. The Cervantes prize, though more prestigious, is awarded for a lifetime's achievement in any form of literature—the novel, drama, as well as poetry.

2. José Kozer, "Esto (también) es Cuba, Chaguito" in *La voracidad grafómana: José Kozer, critica, entrevistas y documentos*, ed. Jacobo Sefamí (Mexico: Universidad Nacional Autónoma de Mexico, 2002), 25. The translation here, and wherever not otherwise attributed, is my own.

3. Ibid., 23.

4. Ibid., 25.

5. This is not meant to imply any rejection by the individual poets mentioned here of neobaroque poets in general. Álvaro Mutis, for example, greatly admired Kozer's poetry, as shown in his review of *Bajo este cien* (Mutis, 313–15). Respect between accomplished poets of different approaches and schools, and the recognition that powerful poetry can be achieved in diverse ways, is far more widespread than generally implied in literary histories.

6. Although these remarks on the differences between poetry in the Spanish and English traditions are based on conversations with Latin American poets and readers of poetry as well as my own reading, they owe much to the analysis by Yves Bonnefoy of the differences between the French and English poetic traditions, in particular differing attitudes to the role of concrete detail and description in poetry. See in particular "Shakespeare and the French Poet" and "French Poetry and the Principle of Identity" in Yves Bonnefoy, *The Act and the Place of Poetry: Selected Essays*, ed. John T. Naughton (Chicago: The University of Chicago Press, 1989), 10–20, 118–36.

7. Though born in Peru, Jiménez has lived in Argentina most of his life and considers himself an Argentine poet.

8. For those, like myself, who have been fortunate enough to hear Zurita read, it is an astonishing experience, as if he were channeling the dead of Chile. His work is a clear refutation of the idea that neobaroque poetry involves an abandonment of the political or that only a simplistic, one-dimensional poetry can find a mass audience.

9. José Kozer, personal communication via e-mail, December 12, 2016.

10. *Real Academia Española*, s. v. "indole," http://www.rae.es/diccionario-de-la-lengua-espanola/la-23a-edicion-2014.

11. Michel de Montaigne, *The Complete Essays*, 1017–37.

12. Leymen Pérez, "José Kozer: la otra patria," 16–22.

A Note on Sources

The biography of José Kozer presented here is based on the several interviews in *La voracidad grafómana* (2002), particularly the interview with José Homero (83–89) and the interview "Signos del destierro" supplied by Kozer (91–99), as well as the extensive interview with Jacobo Sefamí in *De la imaginación poética* (2013, 251–320), supplemented by additional comments from José Kozer.

Of the several critical essays gathered in the collection *La voracidad grafómana* (2002), those by Jacobo Sefamí (189–230), Miguel Cabrera (121–32), and Eduardo Espina (285–304) were especially useful in developing my sense of the interrelationship between the stylistics of Kozer and the content of his poetry.

Works Cited

Bonnefoy, Yves. *The Act and the Place of Poetry: Selected Essays*. Edited by John T. Naughton. Chicago: The University of Chicago Press. 1989.

Borges, Jorge Luis. *Selected Prose*. Edited and translated by Eliot Weinberger. New York: Penguin Books. 1992.

Cabrera, Miguel. "La armonía (amor): los campos florecidos." In *La voracidad grafómana: José Kozer, critica, entrevistas y documentos*, edited by Jacobo Se-famí, 121-32. Mexico: Universidad Nacional Autónoma de Mexico. 2002.

Echavarren, Roberto, Kozer, José, and Sefamí, Jacobo, eds. *Medusario: Muestra de Poesía Latinoamericana*. Mexico City: Fondo de Cultura Económica, 1996.

Espina, Eduardo. "El silencio leído en voz alta." In *La voracidad grafómana: José Kozer, critica, entrevistas y documentos*, edited by Jacobo Sefamí, 285–304. Mexico: Universidad Nacional Autónoma de Mexico, 2002.

"Índole, noun." In *Diccionario de la lengua Española* (twenty-third edition). Real Academia Española: Madrid (2014). Accessed December 21, 2016. http://www.rae.es/diccionario-de-la-lengua-espanola/la-23a-edicion-2014.

Kozer, José. Personal communcation via e-mail. December 12, 2016.

———. *Tokonoma*. Translated by Peter Boyle. Exeter: Shearsman. 2014.

———. *Anima*. Translated by Peter Boyle. Exeter: Shearsman. 2011.

———. *Tokonoma*. Madrid: Ediciones Amargord. 2011.

———. *Acta*. Mexico: Editorial Aldus. 2010.

———. *Stet: Selected Poems*. Translated by Mark Weiss. New York: Junction Press. 2006.

———. *Y del esparto la invariabilidad*. Madrid: Visor. 2005.

———. *Carece de causa*. 2nd edition. Buenos Aires: tsé=tsé. 2004.

———. *Ánima*. Mexico City: Fondo de Cultura Económica. 2002.

———. "Esto (también) es Cuba, Chaguito." In *La voracidad grafómana: José Kozer, critica, entrevistas y documentos*, edited by Jacobo Sefamí, 15–27. Mexico: Universidad Nacional Autónoma de Mexico, 2002.

———. *La garza sin sombra*. Barcelona: Llibres de Mall. 1985.

———. *Bajo este cien*. Mexico City: Fondo de Cultura Económica. 1983.

———. *Jarrón de las abreviaturas*. Mexico: Premia. 1980.

———. *Y así tomaron posesión en las ciudades*. Barcelona: Ámbito Literario. 1978.

———. *Este judío de números y letras*. Tenerife: Nuestro Arte. 1975.

———. *Padres y otras profesiones*. New York: Ediciones Villamiseria. 1972.

Montaigne, Michel de. *The Complete Essays*. Translated by M. A. Screech. London: Penguin Classics. 2003.

Mutis, Álvaro. "Bajo este cien." In *La voracidad grafómana: José Kozer, critica, entrevistas y documentos*, edited by Jacobo Sefamí, 313–15. Mexico: Universidad Nacional Autónoma de Mexico. 2002.

Pérez, Leymen. "José Kozer: la otra patria." *La Jiribilla Revista de cultura cubana* 615 (February 2013): 16–22. http://www.lajiribilla.cu/articulo/3631/jose-kozer-la-otra-patria.

Sefamí, Jacobo. *De la imaginación poética: conversaciones con Enrique Molina, Gonzalo Rojas, Olga Orozco, Álvaro Mutis, José Kozer y David Huerta*. São Paulo: Lumme Editores. 2013.

———. *La voracidad grafómana: José Kozer, critica, entrevistas y documentos*. Mexico: Universidad Nacional Autónoma de Mexico. 2002.

———. "Llenar la máscara con las ropas del lenguaje: José Kozer." *La voracidad grafómana: José Kozer, critica, entrevistas y documentos*, edited by Jacobo Sefamí, 189–230. Mexico: Universidad Nacional Autónoma de Mexico. 2002.

Sheringham, Michael. *Everyday Life*. Oxford: Oxford University Press. 2006.

Photograph of José Kozer at the University of Virginia in Charlottesville, Virginia, taken on September 19, 2016; courtesy of Eduardo Montes-Bradley

Of Such a Nature / Índole

Véase como a fin de cuentas acaba en empate

Ah Shelley, no doy con la Mente Universal, las
   singularidades de la mente
   me trocan. Palpitaciones.
   Inapetencia. Diarreas. No
   tiene remedio, a mis años
   nada cambia, mejor así,
   iría para peor. No he
   conseguido sujetar a
   uno siquiera de los siete
   demonios que desde
   joven me azuzan, tenía
   a la vista la estera de
   meditación, el butacón
   del reposo, la noción
   de interioridad, daba un
   paso, extendía el brazo,
   descansaba la frente en
   el cristal de una ventana,
   Oh acto intelectual, y
   todo se me esfumaba.
   Nada entiendo. Veo lo
   que ve de inmediato el
   cangrejo al salir de la
   cueva, granos de arena
   cayendo en una clepsidra,
   clepsidra desfondada,
   agua en el fondo agua
   disolviendo. Veo la
   sombra que ve la
   lagartija deslumbrada
   al escurrirse, santiamén
   de santiamenes, bajo
   la piedra descomunal,
   a un lado del camino.

Wherein it is seen how, when all's said and done, it comes out a draw

Ah Shelley, I don't encounter the Universal Mind, the
     mind's singularities confuse
     me. Palpitations. Loss
     of appetite. Bouts of
     diarrhea. There's no
     cure, at my age nothing
     changes, better that
     way, it'd only be for the
     worse. I've not managed
     to subjugate even one of
     the seven demons bugging
     me since youth, I saw
     the meditation mat before
     me, the restful easy chair,
     the idea of inwardness, I
     took a step, stretched out
     my arm, rested my
     forehead on a window
     pane, Oh intellectual
     feat, and everything
     vanished. I understand
     nothing. I see what
     a crab sees immediately
     on leaving its cave, grains
     of sand falling in a
     clepsydra, a bottomless
     clepsydra, in its depths
     water dissolving
     water. I see the
     shade the dazzled lizard
     sees as it darts, quicker
     than the blink of an eye,
     under an enormous rock by

La piedra oculta, no
protege. No sé nada,
en verdad. Todas las
tardes leo (**Hymn to
Intellectual Beauty**)
retina inutilizada, y la
cabeza, como suele
decirse (o al menos
se decía en Cuba)
un colador. Vestigios
de la Nada, sus
segundos vestigios,
grumos desmoronándose
en la sequedad de este
tramo final, a fin de
cuentas, general, poco
tiene que importunar
mis noches. ¿Se nota
que soy filósofo? ¿Mente
intelectual? Me ha dado
otra vez por ponerme
tirantes, me quedan
cortos los pantalones,
ora cuelgan, ora me
están estrechos. Ahí
en el ropero se ven
los tres pares de
mezclilla desleída,
los distingo, distingo
el cuerpo que cubren,
participan de la
insustancia. De la
inmateria. Mera
hechura, catadura
de la tela (del cuerpo).
Si me los pongo al

the roadside. The rock
hides, it doesn't protect.
In truth, I don't know
anything. One afternoon
after another I read (Hymn
to Intellectual Beauty) my
retina useless, and my
head, as it's said (or at
least used to be said in
Cuba) a sieve. Remnants
of Nothingness, its
secondary traces,
lumps crumbling
away in the dryness of the
final stretch, in the end, in
general, not much
reason to disturb
my nights. Can you
tell I'm a philosopher? An
intellectual mind? I'm
wearing suspenders
again, my pants
have grown short,
now they're hanging
loose, now tight. There
in the wardrobe you
see three pairs of
faded jeans, I
can see them, can see
the body they cover,
they share in
the insubstantial. In the
immaterial. Pure
handiwork, the fabric's
(body's) appearance.
If I put them on inside

revés vislumbro la
radiografía de mis
huesos. Y peor, un
sistema nervioso al
borde del colapso.
Ah la muerte, leda
Muerte, impostura
también. Al diablo
con la vida parejera,
se largue por donde
vino, se abisme en
el fétido albañal.
Crucifixión astral. Y
cabe Dios, Nada.
Lento desplomarse,
ved la luna menguante
como opaca al sol que
se afana por estorbar
la nocturnidad. Abuela,
¿qué traes esta tarde
en la bandeja de hierro
forjado que se me
corra de nuevo la baba?
Baba, baba, abuela. Me
acerco al jarrón, prímulas
primeras, unas de plástico,
otras de trapo. ¿Suficiente?
El velo del desconocimiento
cae, ah, verdad manifiesta,
ahora veo llegar la oruga
verde avanzando ciega
sobre el mantel churrioso
de la mesa del comedor:
tiene hambre, yo cuento
con mi hambre dentro
de esta inapetencia

out I glimpse my bones in
x-ray. And worse, a nervous
system on the edge of
collapse. Ah death, easeful
Death, an imposter
as well. To hell with
cheeky life, let it go
back where it came
from, let it sink in
its foul sewer. Astral
crucifixion. And at God's
side, Nothingness.
A slow collapse,
see the waning moon
darkening the sun
as it tries to disturb the
night hours. Grandmother,
what have you got tonight
on the wrought iron tray
that has me drooling?
Drool, drool, granny. I
come close to the vase, the
first cowslips, some
plastic, others
cloth. Enough?
The veil of unknowing
falls, ah, truth made
manifest, now I see the
green caterpillar
arrive moving blindly
forward on the dirty
tablecloth in the
dining room: it's hungry,
I'm counting on my hunger
inside this present lack of
appetite. Both of us

actual. Ambos (dos
seres mecánicos)
contemplamos de
cerca, desganados
(en el fondo tributarios)
hoja de morera, pan
bazo.

(two mechanical
beings) contemplate
close up, apathetic
(in our depths
tributaries)
mulberry leaf, brown
bread.

Véase como el amoroso hijo no olvida la presencia del padre

Heno,
tusa,
a
la

boca: soy equino, res. Hace treinta años que
    murió mi padre (a punto de
    caramelo, yo): me alcanza
    un puñado de

violetas
(refresca
el
aliento)
unas

amapolas (verás se te ponen los ojos a
    cuadros) me alimento
    de sus hombros, su
    envejecida clavícula,
    trago aquel aliento a
    amoníaco, nicotina,
    sus dedos tocados
    de ácido úrico
    acarician mis
    chupadas mejillas,
    soy feliz un instante
    antes de

conciliar
el
sueño
al
pie
de

Wherein it is seen how a loving son doesn't forget the presence of the father

Hay,
corncob
in
my

mouth: I am equine, cattle. It's thirty years since my father
        died (me next, some
        treat, I'm sure): he
        hands me a fistful of

violets
(refreshes
the
breath)
a
few

poppies (you'll see they make your eyes pop right out)
        I nourish myself
        on his shoulders, his
        aged clavicle, I
        swallow that breath
        of ammonia, of nicotine,
        his fingers touched by
        uric acid caress my
        gaunt cheeks, for a
        moment I'm happy
        before going

to
sleep
at
the
foot
of

la Roca donde reposan Rebeca Sara Ana
    Jacob David, las barbas
    de Abrahán farfolla
    reseca, su barrigón

una
hilera
van
y
vienen
de insectos (cornalina turmalina jade):
    santificados nunca
    serán polvo óseo ni
    ceniza, sólo guijarro
    pulverizado por el
    paso de los camellos
    sedientos de sus
    camellas, mundo
    trastocado, necesitado

de
hecatombes.
Hecatombes:
irles
a
la
yugular, ser el más guapo del barrio, y un
    quita y pon perpetuo
    de sabandijas, saco
    a flote la cabeza, me
    alejo a

hurtadillas
del
tremedal,
y

the Rock where rest Rebecca Sara Ana Jacob
David, Abraham's beard
a dry husk, his potbelly

a
thread
the
coming
and
going
of insects (carnelian tourmaline jade):
sanctified they will
never be ash or
bone dust, only pebbles
ground down by the
passage of camels
thirsting for their
she-camels, a world
turned upside down,
in need of

hecatombs.
Hecatombs:
go
for
the
jugular, be the neighborhood bully, and
eternal replaceable part
of the general scum, my
head surfaces, quietly
I step away from

the
seething
quagmire
and

voy cediendo una a una mis ilusiones, lo irreal
    me volvió irreal, me
    alimento de maloja,
    bebo agua lustral,
    vetusta, de unas

pozas
del
camino
a

¿Roma, Jerusalén, Santiago? En el camino a
    mi nueva casa los
    muertos se aparean,
    me refiero a los
    menos viejos, y yo
    entro, me quito el
    saco de yute, le
    prendo (según
    el ritual) fuego
    (inclemente)

y
para
siempre
me
siento
a

lo de siempre, leer letras góticas, canturrear
    músicas sacras (barítonos)
    he alcanzado la forma de
    la res, a medias centauro,
    a medias de mi padre soy
    antebrazo: la proximidad
    de sus dedos llagados
    de eccema me convoca,

one by one give up my illusions, things unreal have
        turned me unreal, I
        nourish myself on
        corn husks, drink
        venerable, lustral
        waters from certain

puddles
along
the
road
to

Rome, Jerusalem, Santiago? On the road to my new
        house the dead
        fornicate, I'm
        referring to the
        least old, and I enter,
        take off my jute
        dress jacket, set
        it (following the
        ritual) on (un-
        forgiving) fire

and
for
ever
I
sit
with

the same old same old, read gothic script, sing sotto voce
        sacred music (baritones)
        I've achieved the shape
        of cattle, half centaur,
        half my father's

constato sus caricias por
las bascas

y
la
duración
de
mis
arcadas.

forearm: the closeness
of his fingers pained
by eczema summons me,
I prove his caresses by
my bouts of nausea

and
the
duration
of
my
retching.

Véase como el oficial de marina no nos revela su vida secreta

Cinco minutos deshaciendo el nudo, soltó las
    amarras, el bote se alejó
    de la orilla izquierda con
    sus casas blancas, tejas
    rojas, la casa de tejas
    negras desaparece tras
    el primer recodo: un río
    ancho, navegable en
    toda su extensión hasta
    el fin del mundo, hasta
    el día del Juicio: se puso
    el traje marcial de la Gran
    Guerra, oficial de infantería
    de marina, un distintivo en
    la gorra negra, rayas
    blancas, visera escarlata:
    y dos medallas en la
    solapa izquierda, la
    amarilla fue oro, la de
    cobre color cardenillo:
    medalla de plata, oro y
    platino, bueno, siempre
    supo cómo y a quiénes
    se otorgan.

Rema. Alza los remos, la vertical (chorrea) al
    sol implacable, ni una
    sombra en la distancia
    ni en la superficie del
    agua: ya era hora que
    los remos no arrojaran
    sombras. Detuvo el
    discurrir. De las aguas,
    por sí: aguas lentas.
    De las aves, en esta

Wherein it is seen how the navy officer does not reveal his secret life to us

Five minutes untying the knot, he cast off, the boat moved
     away from the left shore
     with its white houses, red
     tiles, the house of black
     tiles vanishes after the
     first bend: a deep river,
     navigable in all its length as
     far as the end of the world,
     as Judgment Day: he has
     put on the military
     uniform of the Great
     War, an officer in the
     Marines, an emblem on
     the black cap, white
     stripes, scarlet visor: and
     two medals on the left
     lapel, the yellow one was
     gold, the copper-colored
     verdigris: a medal of silver,
     gold and platinum, then,
     he always knew how and
     to whom they are
     awarded.

He rows. He lifts the oars, the upright one (drips) in the
     relentless sun, not one
     shadow in the distance
     or on the water's
     surface: it was about
     time oars cast no
     shadows. He stopped
     the flow of thought.
     About the waters, *per*
     se: slow waters. About the

mañana de calor estival
bogando (comienza la
primavera, los almendros
florecieron, florecerán
las hileras de cerezos)
(a lo lejos): y de sus
pensamientos. Lo asaltan;
los ataja. Canturrea los
primeros versos de un
sutra que repite para
sus adentros, cada vez
más adentro, hace años.

Marino. Toda una vida secreta. Permaneció
soltero. Hizo caso omiso
del reglamento y del
mundo, se escabulló.
No cultivó pasada la
adolescencia sus
inquietudes intelectuales,
leía toneladas de libros,
conocimiento que
descartaba. Un buen
día (para ser precisos,
una cierta tarde, al
anochecer) dejó de
leer. Sopetón. Malbarató
o regaló sus libros.
Primeras ediciones
(Conrad, sobre todo)
libros firmados, incunables
comprados a precio de
oro, y su colección de
estatuillas africanas:
pegó candela a cartas,
cuadernos, libretas, el
ojo que todo lo anota,

birds, on this morning of
summer heat rowing
(spring is beginning, the
almond trees have
flowered, the rows of
cherry trees will flower)
(in the distance); and
about his thoughts. They
assault him, he cuts them
off. He softly intones the
first verses of a
sutra he's repeated
inwardly, each time more
inwardly, for years.

A sailor. An entire life kept secret. He has remained a
bachelor. Has ignored
regulations and the
world, has escaped.
After adolescence he
didn't cultivate his
intellectual curiosity, he
used to read mountains
of books, knowledge he'd
dismiss. One fine day (to
be precise, a certain
afternoon, at sunset) he
stopped reading. Out of
the blue. Sold off his
books cheap or gave
them away. First
editions (Conrad,
most of all) signed
books, incunabula he'd
paid for dearly, and
his collection of
African figurines: set

correspondencia amorosa,
salió al día siguiente por
primera vez, hasta el fin
del mundo, el día del
Juicio, a pescar. Lucios

y
tencas,
uno
y
una,
desayuno
(pez
ahumado)
y
cena
(rodaja
de
lucio
sin
una
espina)
agua
de
manantial
conservada
en
damajuana:
de
los
sus
ojos
llorando,
Oh
ninfas
de
Judea,

fire to his letters, note-
books, diaries, the
eye that jots it all down,
love letters, the next
day he set off for the
first time, towards the
end of the world, to
Judgment day, to
fish. Pike

and
tench,
one
pike
and
one
tench,
breakfast
(smoked
fish)
and
dinner
(sliver
of
pike
without
bones)
spring
water
kept
in
a
demijohn:
with
these
his
eyes

otra
noche
viendo
entrar
de
dos
en
dos
en
hilera
a
los
fiscales.

he
wept,
Oh
nymphs
of
Judaea,
another
night
watching
the
prosecutors
file
in
two
by
two.

Véase como siempre acaba en lo mismo

Un jueves, y no es éste, metí las manos
    en los bolsillos (perdí
    la noción del tiempo).
    De pie, y luego sentado
    en penumbra, y luego a
    oscuras. Ayuné. Bebí
    agua mental. Sabía que
    al amanecer era viernes,
    y con eso me bastaba.
    A veces sacaba las
    manos de los bolsillos,
    puños crispados. Abría
    las manos, todo seguía
    igual. Eso no está mal.
    Surgía, iba surgiendo
    o iba a surgir un
    pensamiento, eso
    no está tampoco mal.
    Uno, y no tres asuntos
    entrecruzándose,
    alterando el ritmo de
    la respiración. Aparecía
    yo aquella tarde en un
    pinar, dunas en la
    distancia, la bahía
    refulgente (cabrilleos)
    (rielar pronto la luna
    llena) (ah el poema
    de Espronceda que
    memoricé durante la
    adolescencia) levanté
    el brazo, extendí la
    mano, se vino a posar
    un paro carbonero,
    ¿seré San Francisco?

Wherein it is seen how it always ends up the same

A Thursday, and not this one, I put my hands in my
pockets (I lost the
concept of time).
Standing, and then
sitting in half-
light, then
darkness. I fasted. I
drank mental
water. I knew at
dawn it would be
Friday, and that was
enough for me.
Sometimes I took my
hands out of my pockets,
fists tightened. I'd open
my hands, all continued
the same. That's not bad.
A thought arose, went on
arising or was about to
arise, that too isn't bad.
One subject, not three
interwoven subjects that
would alter the breath's
rhythm. I appeared that
afternoon in a pine grove,
dunes in the distance, the
bay shining (glittering)
(soon the full
moon glimmers) (ah
Espronceda's poem
I memorized in
adolescence) I raised
my arm, stretched out
my hand, a tit
came and perched, am I

Y la rapaz se quería
posar en mi cabeza
recién tonsurada, la
tonsura la produjo
un rayo. ¿Sería yo
uno de los elegidos,
aquél que convertiría
al ave de carroña en
paloma buchona?
Volvía a meter los
puños en los bolsillos,
a quedarme quieto, tengo
a la mano hace horas el
libro de los 50 poemas
de Osip Mandelstam en
la traducción de Meares,
me he propuesto ayunar,
no leer, tener el menor
número de pensamientos,
realizar el menor número
posible de movimientos
durante dos días. No
está mal. Han pasado
unas 36 horas, y ahora
empiezo a brincar
(mental) de un sitio a
otro, mi madre desde
el Más Allá me anima
a volver a la normalidad,
y mi padre, el ceño
fruncido, los brazos
cruzados sobre el pecho
(modelo otomano) o cual
si fuera un campeón de
lucha libre, me contempla
como aquél que contempla
a un pobre diablo a todas

Saint Francis?
And a bird of prey
wanted to settle on my
recently tonsured head, a
jolt of lightning left it
tonsured. Am I one of the
elect, the one to convert
the carrion bird to a
pouter pigeon? Again
I put my fists in my
pockets, stay still, for
hours I keep right next
to me the book
50 poems by Osip
Mandelstam in the
Meares translation, I've
planned to fast, not to
read, to entertain the
smallest number of
thoughts, make the least
possible number of
movements for two
days. That's not bad.
Some 36 hours have
passed, and now I begin
to jump about (mentally)
from one place to another,
my mother in the
Beyond urges me to
come back to normality,
and my father, brows
knitted, arms folded on
chest (ottoman-style) or
as if he was a champion
wrestler, looks at me like
someone contemplating
a poor devil obviously

luces incapacitado para
la vida. ¿Y él; y él? Callo.
No rebatirlo. Eso estaría
mal. En eso consiste en
caer en la trampa. No
ponerme, después de
dos días de interioridad,
mínima actividad motriz,
a disputar. Con él. Ni
con nadie. Ni con el
otomano ahí enfrente,
ni con el zahorí que
me indica el camino
del agua con pozos
que serán la riqueza
de Israel. ¿Y por qué
no de Andalucía?
Amanece. Llevo
horas desvelado.
Soy un enredador
enredado en sus
minucias, los sucesos
del día. Todo una vez
más me afecta. Que si
tal que si esto que si
aquél dijo o dejó qué
de decir. ¿Eh? El
viento viene de los
Urales, el olor a lejía
de las lavanderas del
Caspio, y los rostros
descompuestos son
un asunto, fíjate,
entre mi padre y yo.

unfit for life. And him; what
about him? I say nothing.
Offer him no refutation. That
would be bad. Would mean
falling into the trap. After
two days of
inwardness, minimal
motor function, I'm not
starting an argument. With
him. Or anyone. Not even
with the ottoman there in
front of me, or the diviner
who points me to the
path of the waters with
wells that will be the
wealth of Israel. And why
not Andalusia?
Dawn. I have been up for
hours without sleep. I am
a tangler tangled
up in his minutiae, the
day's events. Everything
affects me over and over.
What if this person or that
person or the other said
or left unsaid something
what to say. Eh? The
wind blows from the
Urals, scent of bleach
from washerwomen of
the Caspian, and their
distorted faces are a
matter for discussion,
imagine that, between
my father and me.

Véase como siempre soterrado en mí hay un judío

Baladas
gemir,
canto
llano

oír en lo adelante, constante, hasta el final.
    Espigas hollar el día
    del Juicio Final, y ver
    brotar de moldes
    inasibles pan candeal.
    Del

olmo
ajeno
a
toda

representación, sin ser una aparición, divisarse,
    y no es portento, la
    pera bergamota,
    caudal. De agua.
    A la boca. Morder
    y entornar los ojos.
    Un silencio sagrado
    nimbe a los

comensales:
tal
que
soy

Wherein it is seen how buried always inside me is a Jew

To
howl
out
ballads,

to hear plainchant up ahead, constantly, right to the end.
    To tread ears of corn
    on Judgment Day, and
    see wholegrain bread
    emerge from un-
    graspable trays.
    On the

elm
foreign
to
all

representation, without being an apparition, to make out,
    and this no miracle, a
    juicy desert pear, its
    wealth. Of water.
    Brought to the mouth.
    To bite, eyes half
    closed. A holy
    silence haloes those
    gathered at the

table:
such
that
I
am

madre. Y veo llegar al padre de los altos hornos
　　con su mandil de cuero
　　y las tenazas calientes
　　en el bolsillo del curtido
　　delantal

que
todavía
nos
sobrecoge.

A los tres. Y a él. La madre sirve en las ventas
　　del camino, el padre
　　forja en un crisol de
　　vidrio a la salida de
　　los pueblos, padres

ambulantes,
hijos
de
una

diáspora diaria a la que nos acostumbrara, iba
　　a decir Dios, pero son
　　cosas de la Historia.
　　Del ángel de tinieblas
　　que a veces se
　　transforma en

exterminador.
En
casa
aprendimos

mother. And I see father come from the blast furnaces with his
        leather apron and the
        hot tongs in the
        pocket of the hardened
        smock that

still
holds
us
in
awe.

The three of us. And him. Mother serves in roadside
        inns, father forges in
        a glass crucible at the
        exit of villages, wandering

parents,
sons
of
a

daily diaspora which they are made accustomed to by, I
        was going to say God, but
        these are matters of
        History. Of the angel
        of darkness that
        sometimes transforms to

exterminator.
At
home
from
childhood
on

desde pequeños a comer peras del olmo, el pan
    sin levadura se lo damos a los
    puercos y los puercos se los
    vendemos a los

vecinos.
Somos
(lo
dice

la canción) mercaderes barbados que hablamos
    a medias (entremezclados)
    seis a siete idiomas, y
    descansamos (parte de
    nuestra capacidad de
    simulación) los

domingos.
Vengan
ferias
que

estamos muertos a la alegría, al atavío del
    Príncipe y la doncella
    casta, somos traperos,
    vivimos

en
la
lengua
oculta

entre oficios bajos. El león y la oveja para
    los demás: para
    nosotros el

we learnt to eat pears from elms, we feed unleavened
    bread to the pigs and
    sell the pigs to the

neighbors.
We
are
(so

the song says) bearded merchants who speak half-half (mixed
    together) six or
    seven languages, and
    we rest (part of our
    knack for feigning) on

Sundays.
Bring
on
the
festivals
where

we are dead to joy, to the robes of the
    Prince and the chaste
    maid, we are rag and
    bone people, we live

in
a
language
hidden

among lowly trades. Let the rest have the
    lion and the lamb:
    for us the filthy

churrioso talego
con la moneda
dorada para
entrar

en
el
Más
Allá.

Por mi parte, hasta el final, en las mezclas,
        cantaré para la
        Novia coplas del
        Sefarad, haré
        para irnos la

maleta
(soga
y
cartón):

de acopio la ilusión de nuevas tierras, a fin
        de cuentas el Mesías,
        en fin, ayudo cuento
        puedo a rellenar

en
casa
las
coles.

sack with the
golden coin to
enter

into
the
Beyond.

For my part, till the end, among all the mixtures, I
    will sing for the
    Beloved couplets
    of Sefarad, so
    we can leave I
    will pack the

suitcase
(cardboard
and
rope):

in abundant supply dreams of new lands, at the end of the
    day the Messiah,
    anyway, here at
    home, I help
    I count I

can
stuff
the
cabbages.

Véase como todo tiene su solución

Hay quien me señala el camino a Oriente, quien
    insiste me quede en el
    sur. Está el asunto de
    las incertidumbres
    económicas, un
    asunto de familia,
    al menos las pérdidas
    se han estabilizado, y
    aunque las cuentas no
    cuadran, y la idea de
    un saldo a favor es
    un auténtico sueño,
    quizás tomando el
    camino de Oriente,
    mercar, volverme
    marrullero, resuelva
    la situación. Al menos
    en parte, tal vez en
    buena parte, y si no
    del todo, más adelante,
    sin estar boyantes,
    nuestra situación de
    familia será holgada.
    Siempre no obstante
    hay un tercer camino,
    nada que ver con
    puntos cardinales ni
    los lugares, un camino
    poblado de florestas,
    animales domésticos
    que conviven con el
    elefante mítico de los
    hindúes, bicéfalos y
    bicharracos que están
    por recibir de Adán sus

Where it is seen how everything has its solution

Someone points me out the road to the East, someone else insists
    I stay in the
    south. It's a matter
    of financial un-
    certainties, a family
    matter, at least the
    losses have settled down,
    and though the figures
    don't add up, and the idea
    of a favorable balance
    is a hopeless dream,
    maybe taking the road
    East, trading, coming
    back a smooth
    talker, might solve the
    situation. At least in
    part, maybe a large
    part, further down
    the track, without
    being prosperous, our
    family situation will
    be ok. Always nonethe-
    less there is a third
    road, nothing to do with
    cardinal points or places,
    a road dense with forests,
    household animals living in
    harmony with the mythic
    elephant of the Hindus,
    two-headed creatures and
    tiny crawling creatures
    waiting to get their
    names from Adam: and from
    French savants imbued
    with encyclopedic ideas,

nombres: y de algún
sabio francés imbuido
de ideas enciclopedistas,
una clasificación completa.
Este camino tiene una
ventaja, el que lo transita
jamás tropieza con
revueltas ni recodos que
lo conducen por otras
sendas. Es posible
sentarse, incluso hallar
asentamiento permanente,
casa, casucha, cueva,
palafito, en alguna que
otra ocasión aposento
interior dentro de un
Palacio (con concubina
y todo). Palacio no es
Paraíso pero al menos
se come, se duerme
tranquilo, se puede
contar con el calor de
una dama de esmerado
entrenamiento. Un
entrenamiento de
bigotes. ¿Qué se hizo
de la familia, qué fue
del problema económico
que nos quitaba el
sueño? Al alba, desde
hace meses, me pica
la cabeza, al rascarme
cae arena, una arena
a veces negra, a veces
rubia. ¿Cómo se llama
el animal que en caso
de necesidad esconde

a complete classification.
This road has one
advantage, if you follow
it you never run into
any twists or sharp
turns that lead you to other
paths. It's possible to
sit down, even find a
permanent settlement,
a house, a hovel, a cave, a
shack on stilts, from
time to time the
inner bedchamber of
a Palace (with a
concubine and
everything). A Palace
isn't Paradise but at least
you can eat, sleep
calmly, count on the
warm affection of a woman
with meticulous
training. Top class
training. What happened to
the family, to the
financial problem that
stole our sleep? For months
now at dawn my
head stings, when I
scratch it sand falls, a
sometimes black
sometimes blond sand.
What's the name for
the animal that in
moments of necessity
hides its head in
sand? Is it a flying

la cabeza en la arena?
¿Es un volátil? ¿Ñandú,
marabú? ¿Ágil pez, ave
lira que no canta? He
visto la luz, todo ha sido
pura neurastenia cuándo
no de mi parte. Aflojo.
Aflojo. Me desentiendo.
Desde un mirador veo
pasar bandadas de
estorninos que el Señor
alimenta desde las
páginas de la Biblia,
los pájaros no se ven
preocupados, no andan
por ahí divulgando a
los cuatro vientos su
situación, pasan
(pasaron) volvieron.

bird? The Greater Rhea, a
marabou stork? A
flying fish, a lyrebird
that doesn't sing? I've
seen the light, it's all
been pure neurasthenia
as when isn't it with me?
I slow down. I slow
down. I avoid things. From
a balcony I see bands of
starlings fly by that
the Lord feeds according
to the Bible, the birds don't
look worried, they don't
go about divulging their
situation to the four
winds, they pass by
(have passed by) they've
come back.

Véase cuánto ocurre a una mujer a solas en un par de horas

Suspensa

ante el plato de sopa de avena (sopla) vuelve
    a estar suspensa (espera)
    no piensa: no actúa más
    allá de la presencia del
    hambre nada excesiva
    que experimenta ora de
    mañana, ora al mediodía
    (a la noche nunca cena):
    agarra la cuchara sopera,
    la mira (acto contemplativo)
    al fiel la sombra metálica
    de la cuchara sobre el
    mantel, junto al cuenco
    sopero de avena: no
    necesita mirar el reloj
    de pared para saber
    que son las siete menos
    cuarto, suspensos están
    los sentidos, sabe que
    la taza de café sobre
    la mesa (mantel de
    hule a cuadros blancos
    verde esmeralda) arroja
    un aroma que la deja
    suspensa, y que el
    olor de la arcilla va
    emanando de la forma
    de la taza: sabe que
    debajo de todo siempre
    hay algo. Hasta tocar
    fondo. Un fondo
    compuesto de planos

Wherein it is seen how much happens in a few hours to a woman on her own

In suspense

before the bowl of oatmeal (she blows) once more
    in suspense (waits)
    doesn't think: takes no
    further action beyond
    the presence of the not
    excessive hunger she
    feels sometimes in the
    morning, sometimes
    at midday (she never
    eats dinner at night): she
    grasps the soup spoon,
    looks at it (a contemplative
    act) balancing the metal
    shadow of the spoon on
    the tablecloth, beside the
    bowl of oatmeal: no
    need to look at the
    clock on the wall to
    know it's a quarter to
    seven, the senses hang
    in suspense, she knows
    the cup of coffee on the
    table (plastic tablecloth
    with white and emerald
    green squares) releases
    an aroma that leaves her
    hanging in suspense, and
    knows the earthy smell
    comes from the cup's
    substance: she knows that
    under everything there's
    always something. Till you

superpuestos, inasequible.
En el fondo y a todos los
efectos, no hay fondo.
Ella es ella, ahí: con
sus características,
sus quehaceres. Jamás
se desfonda. Es un
bulto. Una instancia.
El hecho de ser ella,
ahí. Pronto darán las
siete, recogerá las
dos piezas de vajilla sobre
la mesa, cuenco y taza al
fregadero, hoy toca lavar
a fondo el mantel de hule,
habrá que acercarse al
lavadero de la comunidad,
mucho puño a la hora de
restregar el hule con el
jabón, quitarle la grasa
acumulada de semanas
(tampoco es excesiva):
cuenco y taza secándose
en el escurridor. Y ella,
muerta. O viva. Camino
del lavadero, si nadie la
mira, se podrá contonear
cual si fuera una bayadera
de épocas antiguas. Sus
pechos rozando la tela
del vestido azul de
percal. Sus muslos,
sus especulativas
pudendas rozando la
tela del pantalón de
mezclilla que viste

touch bottom. A deep base
made of superimposed
planes, unreachable. At the
deepest level and to all
intents and purposes, there
is no bottom. She is what
she is, there: with her
characteristics, her chores.
The bottom never falls
out of her life. It's one
package. A moment.
The fact of being herself,
there. Soon it will be
seven, she'll collect the
two pieces of crockery on
the table, a bowl and cup
to the sink, today she must
give the plastic tablecloth
a thorough wash, she'll have
to go to the shared laundry,
hard work scrubbing the
plastic cloth with soap,
getting rid of the weeks'
accumulated grease
(it's not even excessive):
bowl and cup drying in
the drainer. And she herself,
dead. Or alive. On the way
to the laundry, if no one
looks at her, she could
wiggle her hips like a
dancing girl from
ancient times. Her breasts
brushing the fabric of
her dress of blue flimsy
cotton. Her thighs, her
imagined pudenda

debajo del vestido de
percal. Torcaza. Y
una trenza guindando,
oscilando al vaivén de
su cintura, permanece
suspensa. Tiembla
como un pajarito,
descarta la trepidación.
Ya es mujer. Veneranda.
Por otra parte, ataja el
contoneo del cuerpo
rumbo al lavadero,
no hay que herir los
sentimientos de Dios.
Ocho de la mañana.
Canto italiano, el único
que conoce, contempla
a su alrededor la ausencia
generalizada de bienes
materiales, cuelga un
perno de la pared de
la sala, cuelgan unos
vestidos desteñidos del
ropero: en verdad nada
le falta, café (aroma)
avena (se le hace la boca
agua) pan, huevos,
ensalada, para el
almuerzo hay dos
botellas de vino
blanco en la heladera:
nieves en el congelador.
Sus chanclos de madera
para salir son los mismos
que se pone en casa
(rojos) se pone a cantar

brushing the fabric of
the denim pants she
wears under the
flimsy cotton dress.
Turtledove. And her
braids let down, swinging
back and forth to the
rhythm of her waist, hanging
in suspense. She trembles
like a little bird, casts off her
trepidation. Now she
is a woman. Someone
to be worshipped. On the
other hand, she breaks off
the wiggling of her body on
the way to the laundry, no
need to wound God's
feelings. Eight in the
morning. Italian singing,
the only style she
knows, she gazes at the
general absence of material
possessions around her,
a bolt hangs from
the living room
wall, some faded dresses
hang in the wardrobe:
truly nothing's missing,
coffee (its aroma) oats
(they make her mouth
water) bread, eggs,
salad, for lunch there
are two bottles of white
wine in the fridge: iced
sorbet in the freezer.
Her wooden clogs for
going out are the same

a voz en cuello, éstas
son arias de Bach,
morendo, morendo,
modula y acaba (brazos
en jarras) se ve en los
faros, los espejos, a la
altura de las esferas,

suspensa.

she wears in the house
(red ones) she starts
to sing at the top of her
lungs, they are arias
of Bach, *morendo,*
morendo, she adjusts her
voice and finishes
(hands on hips) sees
herself in lighthouses,
mirrors, close to
the spheres, hanging

in suspense.

Véase desde mi punto de vista

Una galleta de arroz integral, mastico, cierro
    los ojos, la galleta está
    intacta, mastico, el
    hambre invariable.

Los grilletes rotos, el muerto que me acompaña
    desde que tengo
    uso de razón, se
    ha desvanecido:
    era una mosca,
    aplasté de
    un pisotón la
    cresa, zumbidos
    desvaneciéndose,
    cantó un gallo.

El gallo era una moneda dorada, aleación de
    metales corrientes: el río
    a la vista (nada acarrea)
    estancado. Un solo
    bote y en el bote (popa)
    dos sombras. El botero
    y su perro. Insulsos.
    Empobrecidos. Un hueso
    a roer, una escudilla con
    gachas de avena. Ambos,
    embrutecidos (¿quién
    come qué?).

Ahora se trata de mí. Acabé de masticar la
    galleta sin sal, el
    hambre se ha
    saciado: hacen
    su entrada el
    botero y el perro,

Wherein it's seen from my point of view

A cracker of brown rice, I chew, I close my eyes, the cracker
    isn't touched, I
    chew, the hunger
    doesn't change.

The broken shackles, the dead man who has accompanied
    me since I reached
    the age of reason, has
    vanished: it was
    a fly, I squashed
    the larva with my
    foot, its buzzing
    ceased, a rooster
    crowed.

The rooster was a golden coin, an alloy of base metals: the
    river in front of us
    (it carries nothing)
    stagnant. A single
    boat and in the boat
    (the stern) two shadows.
    The boatman and his
    dog. Dull. Impoverished.
    A bone to chew, a bowl
    of oatmeal porridge.
    Both, mind-numbingly
    dull (who eats what?)

Now it's about me. I've finished chewing the unsalted
    cracker, my hunger
    is sated: the boatman
    and the dog make
    their appearance,
    you, the closest to
    the inorganic, lie

tú, el más cercano
a lo inorgánico,
échate, y tú,
testaferro de
dioses, a la
cabecera de la
mesa, abre la
boca, muestra la
gandinga, ponte a
dormitar.

Ésta es mi hora. Para siempre y después de
muerto atesoraré estos
días. Inactivo. Compuesto
simple. Unos pocos
pensamientos, un desierto
nada extenso, los mínimos
de la sed y del hambre.
La música viene de casa
de un vecino forofo de
Schubert, el libro abierto
sobre la cama es visible
desde la ventana que
da al sur, a qué hora
volverá a retomar la
lectura. He imaginado.
Empieza a ponerse el
sol. El viento golpea
la contraventana.
Presiento el sueño.
Un sueño ámbar
oloroso a trementina.
El pinar, en mi cabeza
resumir con precisión
los acontecimientos
del día, sus sombras.
Estoy convencido que

down, and you, front
man of gods, at
the head of the
table, open your
mouth, reveal the
inner you (intestines),
apply yourself to
dozing.

This is my hour. Forever and after my death I will
treasure these days.
Inert. A simple
compound. A few
thoughts, a desert
(quite a small one),
minimal amounts
of thirst and hunger.
Music comes from
a neighbor's, a fan
of Schubert, the book
open on the bed is
visible from the
south-facing window,
at what hour will
he return to resume
reading. I've
wondered. The sun
is starting to set. The
wind strikes the shutter.
A presentiment of
sleep. An amber
sleep scented with
turpentine. The
pine forest, to recall
precisely in my head
the day's events, its
shadows. I'm convinced

en un santiamén me
quedaré dormido, en
un santiamén habré
despertado: ya me
veo (azogado)
acercarme a la
despensa, sacar
una galleta de arroz
integral sin sal, el
cuerpo necesita sal.

in one blink of an
eye I'll be asleep, in
another I will have
woken: now I see my
(mercurial) self go
to the pantry, take out
a brown rice cracker
with no salt, the body
needs salt.

Véase desde una sola perspectiva

En el Mar de Amur iré a mojarme los pies
    recién desembarazados
    de la mortaja, sueltos el
    forro y las tablas de pino
    de la caja.

El forro una oveja, las tablas un caserón
    para cobijarme del tiempo
    inclemente que se avecina
    como única constante: pies
    de toba, y en la mirada el
    mármol de las lápidas da
    señales de vida, señales
    petrifican la mirada: las
    aguas grises del Mar de
    Amur, y los vestigios ah
    los vestigios de su mujer
    ataviada de ropa blanca,
    zapatos de lona, el
    casquete de los judíos,
    todavía la oigo leer el
    Sutra del Corazón en
    voz baja, para cuándo
    se lo sabrá de memoria
    y podré yo descansar
    en el lecho (arrecifes)
    del Mar.

Coral, anémonas, enormes esturiones, y de
    sus huevas se van
    deshilvanando unos
    recuerdos, la huida
    a Egipto por países
    Bálticos, patrañas
    de mis padres,

Wherein it is seen from a single perspective

In the Sea of Amur I will go and wet my feet released
    from the shroud just
    now, the lining and
    the box's pine-wood
    planks set free.

The lining a sheep, the planks a big ramshackle house to protect
    me from the inclement
    weather that approaches
    like the sole constant:
    tufa feet, and within
    sight the marble
    tombstones give signs of
    life, signs turn my gaze
    to stone: the grey waters
    of the Sea of Amur, and
    the traces ah the traces
    of his woman dressed in
    white linen, canvas
    runners, skullcap of the
    Jews, yet I can hear her
    softly reading the Heart
    Sutra, when will that
    be known by heart and
    I'll be able to relax on
    the bed (the reefs) of
    the Sea.

Coral, anemones, enormous sturgeon, and from their
    roe a few memories
    unravel and escape,
    the flight into Egypt
    through Baltic
    countries, my parents'
    tall stories, two trans-

dos trasatlánticos
convergen en un
puerto tropical, lo
sucio y lo maloliente
quedaron atrás en
menos de lo que
canta un gallo,
somos ricos (eran
emprendedores mis
padres, por separado
y como pareja, en dos
patadas pudieron
mudarse a un reparto
burgués de las afueras,
una ciudad condenada
de antemano a servir
de experimento social):
no se cansa de fracasar
el ser humano.

Y el devenir, la doble señal de la inquietud
en las sienes, obleas:
yo volveré de casa a
un país Báltico, a Egipto,
a desandar el camino
de mis padres, llegar
(acabo de llegar) a la
orilla extrema de la
Barcaza de incontables
pisos rumbo a: se habla
en cientos de idiomas,
en cuanto llegue nos
harán bajar, parece
que fuéramos a subir,
quién de broma se
atreve a preguntar si
hay ascensor. Chapotean,

atlantic liners meet
in a tropical port, one
filthy, one bad-smelling,
quick as a wink they
stayed behind, we're
rich (they were
entrepreneurs, my
parents, individually and
as a couple, two seconds
flat and they move to a
middle-class neighborhood
out in the suburbs, a city
condemned in advance
to serve as a social
experiment): humans
never get tired of
failure.

And the transformation, the double sign of anxiety on
        their temples, wafers:
        I will return home
        to some Baltic
        country, to Egypt, to
        unwalk the road of my
        parents, to reach (I've just
        reached) the furthest
        shore of the Barge with
        uncountable decks
        towards: hundreds
        of languages are
        spoken, as soon as
        the Barge arrives they'll
        make us get off, it
        seems like we were
        going to board, who
        dares to ask as a joke
        if there's a lift. They

algunos ya chapotean, se
me mojan los pies de
piedra, la vista nublada,
una de dos, o estoy ante
la nube negra detrás de
la que se esconde el
Eterno el Agazapado,
o acabo de llegar a la
cumbre de mi descenso,
no hay Balanza ni puerta
perpendicular de bronce
(pedrería) no hay esa luz
anticipada (inconmensurable)
que haría caer los velos de
la retina, caer las cataratas
al Misterio. Unos últimos
elementos (invariables)
aparecen: la pala, la
tierra mojada, las raíces
entrelazadas, lo cuadrado,
y el largo insecto
apropiándose de la
columna vertebral en
una y otra de cuatro
direcciones.

slosh about, some now
slosh about, my stone
feet are wet, my eyes
cloudy, two possibilities,
either I'm before the black
cloud behind which the
Shrouded Eternal One is
hidden, or I've just
reached the peak of my
descent, there's no
Scale or bronze gate (with
precious stones) standing
upright no anticipated
(immeasurable) light
to let the veils fall
from the retina, to let the
cataracts fall before
the Mystery. A few
last (unchanging)
elements appear:
a spade, damp
earth, tangled roots,
square box, and the large
insect taking over my
spine in both of four
directions.

Véase lo que se escribe escuchando a Górecki, leyendo a Mandelstam

Van pereciendo en el aire, muerte eslabonada.
    Espectros, ínfimo
    aspecto de sus
    sombras, relámpagos
    desapercibidos, en
    cadena van muriendo
    al alejarse: cae la
    sombra, cae un
    coágulo de miel, y
    cae por fin, vestigio
    de vestigios de una
    multitud en el fondo
    temible, la abeja. Del
    enjambre jamás ni una
    huella de las que van
    pereciendo en el aire,
    por la muerte libadas.
    Convocadas, por los
    dioses de las grutas,
    galerías soterradas,
    y a veces en las
    cumbres por las diosas
    de las anfractuosidades:
    yacimientos muertos,
    aguas fecales. Ellas
    que vivieron sometidas
    al polen, coincidiendo
    con la procreación,
    música sagrada libando
    de una flor a florestas,
    almíbares en realidad
    icor escondido en las
    venas de los dioses.
    Mueran, y son dechados

Wherein we see what gets written listening to Gorecki while reading Mandelstam

They are perishing in the air, a collective death. Ghosts,
    faint trace of their
    shadows, unperceived
    lightning bolts, one
    after another they slip
    away and die: darkness
    falls, a congealed
    drop of honey falls, and
    finally, remnant of
    remnants of a
    multitude in the
    fearful depths, the bee
    falls. Of the swarm
    never even a trace of
    those perishing in
    the air, drunk up by
    death. Summoned, by
    the gods of grottoes, sub-
    terranean galleries, and
    sometimes on mountain
    peaks by the goddesses of
    anfractuous places:
    depositions of death,
    fecal waters. The bees
    that lived in thrall to
    pollen, being one with
    procreation, drinking in
    sacred music from
    a greenwood flower,
    syrups that in reality
    are ichor hidden in
    the veins of gods. Let them
    die and become models
    of continuity. The bees.

de continuidad. Las
abejas. Cuánto asombro
las abejas. Son bípedos,
a su manera. Chispazos
de Hefestos, rumores de
Pan en lo más recóndito
de la maleza. Acompañan
a los dioses menores,
los dioses de todas las
índoles. Ahí van a verlos
hacer sus barrabasadas
en lo tupido del bosque.
Son el ojo de un Dios
genital en la piquera
de las colmenas.
Furia a veces, pura
secreción. A veces
moscas empobrecidas
abalanzándose hacia
arriba, a qué, el vuelo
nupcial de transformación.
A tábanos, a moscardón.
A huecos negros donde
desaparecen las celdillas
de una miel hexagonal
que carece de deposición.
Y la anciana del delantal
negro, madejas su
cabellera, cofia
almidonada, ojos zarcos
nublados (ciegos) rojos
zapatos de tacón de
aguja, las mira y las
mira camino del sol
poniente: ora Proserpina,
ora Diana. Las corona.
La anciana. En la

How astonishing bees
are. They're bipeds, in
their own way. Sparks of
Hephaestus, rustling
sounds of Pan in the
scrub's most secret
hiding place. Companions
to minor gods, gods
of all shapes and sorts.
The bees go to watch these
mischief makers in the
dense forest. The eye
of a genital God in the
hives' peephole. Sometimes
a fury, pure secretion.
Sometimes impoverished
flies rushing upwards, to
what, the nuptial flight
of transformation. Into
sandflies, to hornets.
To black holes where
cells of hexagonal
honey disappear, lacking
fresh deposits. And the old
lady with the black
apron, her hair a tangled
mop, starched cap, light
blue clouded (blind)
eyes red stiletto
shoes, looks and
looks at them towards
sunset: at times
Proserpine, at times
Diana. She crowns them.
The old lady. In her
rocking chair. She's going
to crown them later in

mecedora. Irá a
coronarlas después a
otras esferas, ruedo,
corro, círculo concéntrico
de furias sin centro:
enjambre de todas las
especies, y de una sola
criatura. Ahí la taza
humeante de manzanilla,
ahí la anciana removiendo
con cuchara de peltre la
tisana caliente, miel de
ulmo, de romero, de
todas las figuras
incandescentes que
al mediodía arroja su
Rostro: rostro final
agrupado en un
enjambre de abejas,
aguja que perfora el
aire al caer la cofia,
el almidón, caer al
suelo las abejas,
polen derramarse por
la boca. Segregar el sol
(poniente) hormigueros,
la muela de los dioses
de piedra triturando
zumbidos de hollín, del
lapislázuli que fue abeja
y prendedor en la blanca
cabeza de Baucis.

other spheres, ring,
circle, a concentric
circle of furies with no
center: swarm of all
species, and of a single
creature. There the
steaming cup of
chamomile, there
the old lady stirring
the warm tisane
with pewter spoon,
ulmo honey, rosemary
honey, honey of
all incandescent
forms projected by her
Face at midday: a final
face condensed in a
swarm of bees, needle
that pierces the air as
the cap falls, as starch
falls, as bees
fall to the ground,
spilling pollen from their
mouths. Secreting sun
(set) ants' nests, the gods'
millstone grinding out a
whirring of soot, of
lapis lazuli that was bee
and brooch in the blank
head of Baucis.

Véase si todo lo que se dice a continuación alcara algo

Empapado, con sobresalto, de sudor, me falta
   el aire, el reloj de la mesa
   de noche indica que dormí
   quince minutos creyendo
   haber dormido horas. No
   puedo prender la lámpara
   porque la noche castiga a
   quienes la perturban. No
   puedo salir de la cama
   porque los féretros son
   inamovibles. ¿Y adónde
   iría a estas horas? Afuera
   hay unos trescientos
   cerezos secos, una
   guardarraya por la que
   van y vienen toda la noche
   las alimañas, enjambres
   semidormidos de moscas,
   grillos ofuscados que
   permanecen toda la noche
   en una postura egipcia,
   callados. Éste es el silencio
   de las gemas verdes, y del
   trastorno mental. Detrás
   de los grillos hay hileras
   de cigarras en idéntica
   situación. Y ahí aparecen,
   desordenadas (en
   apariencia) hormigas
   negras, las carpinteras,
   las hormigas de fuego:
   no separan el hambre
   incesante de todo el
   día, del hambre de la
   noche. Igual procuro

Wherein it is seen whether all that's said later clarifies anything

Waking with a start, soaked in sweat, I can hardly breathe, the
    clock on the night
    table shows I've slept
    fifteen minutes
    thinking I've slept for
    hours. I can't turn on
    the lamp because
    night punishes those
    who disturb it. Can't
    get out of bed because
    coffins can't be
    moved. And where
    would I go at this hour?
    Outside are some three
    hundred dry cherry
    trees, a track between
    them on which all
    night small bugs
    come and go, swarms
    of half-asleep flies,
    confused crickets that
    stay there all night in an
    Egyptian position, making
    no sound. This is the silence
    of green gems and mental
    confusion. Behind the
    crickets rows of
    cicadas in the same
    situation. And
    (apparently)
    disorganized black ants,
    carpenter ants, fire
    ants that don't
    distinguish the day's

conciliar otra vez el
sueño, puede que lo
consiga, la valeriana,
ciertos fármacos,
qué sé yo. Dormito
(deambulo) probable
me quedé de nuevo
dormido, esta vez a
fondo, abro los ojos,
aumenta mi postración
al ver en el reloj digital
del velador que han
pasado quince minutos.
No sé siquiera si se trata
de los quince minutos de
antes o de otros nuevos
quince minutos. Hurgo
en mí a ver si tengo
hambre. ¿Por qué no
me animo a poner la
luz? ¿Leer? No sé leer.
Hace años que no sé
leer. La noche se ha
incorporado a mi
sustancia (noche
infusa) se derrama
a todo lo largo del
cuerpo, lo reduce a
un continuo martillar
de clavículas, lo óseo
se quiere quebrar en
la noche: clavos largos
herrumbrosos penetran
del aire a la sien. Estoy
amedrentado, es
vetusto el clavo,
sendero de hormigas,

ceaseless hunger from the
night's. Maybe I'll try
once more to get to
sleep, maybe it'll
work, the valerian, certain
drugs, what do I know.
I snooze (mind
wander) probably I've
been asleep again,
this time deeply, I open
my eyes, my exhaustion
increases as I see on
the digital clock on the
night table fifteen
minutes have passed. I
don't even know if
that's the fifteen
minutes from before or
a new fifteen minutes.
I delve into myself to
see if I'm hungry. Why
can't I bring myself
to turn on the light? To
read? I don't know
how to read. For years
I haven't known how
to read. Night has become
part of my substance (an
innate night) it spills
all over my body, reduces
it to one continuous
hammering of my
clavicles, bones want
to break at night: long
rusty nails penetrate
from the air into my
temples. I'm scared, the

silencio de grillos.
Grillete la nocturnidad.
Seduce, ¿pero en qué
punto ajeno a la luz
contiene el ápice de
sueño hasta el fondo?
Cerrar los ojos, olvidar
la idea del sueño,
relegar todo descanso
a otras existencias:
dejarse llevar río abajo,
de candil en candil por
un camino de sirga,
remolcadores de un
solo rumbo cargados
del sobrecogimiento
de los muertos: yo
participo, yo participaré.
y veremos si como se
nos ha dicho, el cuerpo
magullado, según lo
previsto, se ladea a
mirar la hora.

nail's ancient, a path
of ants, silence of
crickets. The night hours
are shackles. Are seductive,
but in what spot foreign to
all light do they hold
the faintest trace of
sleep's depths? To close
the eyes, forget the
idea of sleep, postpone
all rest to other
existences: to let
yourself be carried
downstream, past
candle after candle on
a towpath, tugboats in
a single direction
heavy with the awe of
the dead: I am part
of it, will be part of it. And
let's see if as we've
been told, the bruised
body, as expected,
leans over to look
at the hour.

Véase, hasta para un chino, la imposibilidad de alcanzar la escritura

Yang Wan Li mira las nubes a la altura de
    la mirada, raudas a veces,
    a veces (inalcanzables)
    las ve alejarse a Poniente.

Se incorpora, la grama talló sus espaldas
    (¿será indeleble?): deja en
    sus carnes el ideograma
    nube junto al ideograma
    mirada, y el jeroglífico
    enrojecido, en sus
    orígenes verde, que
    constituye el ideograma
    Poniente.

Lo inscrito es añadidura, altera el Universo. El
    exceso de inteligencia
    preocupa a los dioses,
    un exceso de letras les
    repugna. Yang Wan Li,
    desde su mirada, o tal
    vez desde el ideograma
    mirada, cual samurai
    letrado, desafía el ojo
    único de los dioses:
    fácil es atolondrar al
    dios de cien ojos, difícil
    dejar de supeditarse al
    ojo clínico, en verdad
    inhumano, del dios
    ciclópeo.

Su desafío lo lleva a inscribir las nubes (dos

Wherein it's seen how, even for someone Chinese, it's impossible to understand writing

Yang Wan Li looks at the clouds level with his gaze, sometimes
      rushing past , sometimes
      (unreachable) he sees them
      move away into the West.

He sits up, the grass has engraved his back (will this be
      indelible?): in his flesh it
      leaves the ideogram cloud
      beside the ideogram
      gaze, and the reddened
      hieroglyph, in its origins
      green, that forms
      the ideogram
      West.

What is inscribed is addition, it changes the universe. Excessive
      intelligence worries
      the gods, an excess of
      letters they find
      repugnant. Yang Wan Li,
      from his gaze, or maybe
      from the ideogram gaze,
      as any lettered samurai
      would, challenges the
      unique eye of the gods:
      it's easy to confuse the
      hundred-eyed god, difficult
      to stop being a
      subordinate of the
      clinical eye, in truth the
      inhuman eye, of the
      Cyclopean god.

His defiance leads him to inscribe clouds (two strokes)

trazos) la mirada (propia
y general) los ideogramas
verde (enrojecido) y
Poniente en un pliego
de papel de seda que
a sus cortas miras le
parece indestructible.
Buena suerte Yang
Wan Li, el afán de
perduración nada
tiene que ver con la
realidad de los dioses
ni la consistencia del
Universo.

Señales de otoño. Desde el alto mirador de
la casa Yang Wan Li mira
pasar las bandadas de
pelícanos, los alcatraces
sin trasfondo, grullas,
garzas mudas: ve
transcurrir su propia
existencia, desde
hace años ese otro
enmudecimiento: ¿qué
transcribir? Ya se fueron
los años y las aves.

La letra se arruga, se recoge en ápices, trazas,
sobrantes de la tinta o
del pincel (la mano se
inclina a no corresponder):
una última hoja de la
fronda, flor roja del
hibisco que acaba de
caer. A lo sumo registra
las hormigas de un cáliz,

gaze (his own and gaze
in general) the ideograms
green (reddened) and
West on one sheet of
silk paper which to his
limited intelligence
looks indestructible.
Good luck Yang Wan
Li, the longing for
eternal existence has
nothing to do with the
reality of the gods or the
make up of the
Universe.

Signs of autumn. From his house's high lookout tower
Yang Wan Li watches
flocks of pelicans fly
past, gannets of no
background, cranes,
silent herons: he sees
his own existence pass
by, for years now this
other muteness: what
to write down? Now the
years and the birds have
vanished.

Handwriting crumples, collects as specks, traces, excesses of
ink or brush (the hand
tends towards an
absence of harmony):
one final leaf from the
foliage, a red hibiscus
flower that has just
fallen. At most it records
the ants of a calyx, their

sus fauces sucias de
polen, la boca abierta
un quiste negro.

A lo sumo, y eso con suerte, al enrollar el pliego
de seda, Yang Wan Li
verá de nuevo y para
el inmediato olvido
aparecer (desaparecer)
unas nubes raudas, las
tierras a Poniente de las
que no sabe nada, y la
grama, áspera (tajante)
vejándole sus espaldas.

jaws dirty with
pollen, their open mouth
a black cyst.

At most, and this with luck, as he rolls away the silk sheet, Yang
Wan Li will see again,
see and immediately
forget, the appearance
(disappearance) of a
few clouds rushing by,
Western lands about which
he knows nothing, and
the grass, rough (sharp)
vexing his back.

Véase como se alcanza la felicidad con un poco de imaginación

Ayer los dos en pelota picada comiendo
    croquetas de atún, el
    vino blanco, agua
    de manantial, en
    la percha de roble
    cuelga el traje del
    cortesano, en el
    suelo el guantelete
    de cuero forrado
    en piel de zorro,
    el halcón, la
    ballesta, dos
    croquetas a la
    boca, un buche
    de vino (Chablis)
    (gárgaras): a mi
    Dama le bambolean
    las tetas, a mí me
    cuelga el pito.

En la otra alcándara el traje de mandarín
    que vestirá a la tarde
    mi Dama, coletas
    postizas, el pekinés
    de peluche no hay
    quien lo distinga
    de uno de carne
    y hueso, nada,
    que somos la
    distracción del
    barrio, los hay
    que sacan sus
    sillas de tijera
    a esperar nuestro
    paso del brazo

Wherein it's seen how happiness is achieved with a little imagination

Yesterday the two stark naked eating tuna fish cakes,
    white wine, spring
    water, on the oak-
    wood clotheshorse
    hangs the courtesan's
    dress, on the floor
    the leather gauntlet
    lined with fox skin,
    the falcon, the
    crossbow, two
    fish cakes lifted
    to the mouth, a swig
    of wine (Chablis)
    (gargle): my
    Lady's breasts
    wobble, my dick
    hangs.

On the other clothes rack the Mandarin's costume my
    Lady will wear in the
    evening, fake
    pigtails, no one can tell
    the difference between
    a stuffed toy Pekinese
    and one of flesh and
    blood, no difference,
    we provide some
    distraction for the
    neighborhood, there
    are some who
    pull out their
    folding chairs
    to await us as we
    stroll by arm in arm
    talking of secret loves,

conversando de
amores secretos,
riquezas fabulosas,
sésamos y
abracadabras
a un estado
imperturbable
de felicidad.

Esto porque en el fondo somos gente que ha
alcanzado la simplicidad.
Nos hubiera gustado
persuadir al mundo
del camino a seguir,
por Dios, si es tan
sencillo: dos comidas
al día, a la mesa en
pelotas, tres mudas
vistosas de ropa,
control de gastos,
ingresos suficientes,
y las posesiones
más elementales
de fabricación
casera: un lector
de tabaquería
(función que
mi Dama y yo
alternamos)
leyéndonos, a la
hora de la costura,
los remiendos, la
cochura del pan,
una repostería
sencilla, novelas
de Dumas, Hugo,
Balzac (incluso

fabulous riches, open
sesames and
abracadabras
towards an
imperturbable
state of
happiness.

This because fundamentally we are people who have
    achieved simplicity.
    We would love to
    have persuaded the
    world of the road
    to follow, by
    God, if it's so
    simple: two meals
    a day, stark naked
    at the table, three
    attractive changes of
    clothes, control of
    expenses, sufficient
    income, and the most
    basic homemade
    possessions: a cigar-
    factory reader (a
    function my Lady and
    I alternate) reading
    to each other, while
    sewing, doing
    repairs, a batch of
    bread, some
    simple pastry, novels
    by Dumas, Hugo,
    Balzac (it's even
    got into our heads
    to make our
    own paper).

nos ha dado por
hacer nuestro
propio papel).
Poemas de los
modernistas, los
expresionistas
alemanes, por
estas fechas a
la tarde una
buena tanda de
textos laicos y
sagrados del
Lejano Oriente
(siglos ha) de allá
donde laico y
sagrado es igual.

Nuestro símbolo más preciado es la nuez. El
nogal del patio lo vemos
día a día desde un
recogimiento que
ya quisieran para
sí muchos: un tajo
nada profundo que
pronto cicatriza en
la corteza del nogal
nos permite compartir
un vaso de resina
negra rebajada (la
resina que le dedica
Marina Tsvetayeva
a su amante Sofía
Parnok): lo demás,
coser, cantar, comer
croquetas, pasear
(hay que sacar al
perro no sea que

Poems of the
modernists,
the German
expressionists, on
those days in the
afternoon a
whole stack
of sacred and
secular texts from the
Far East (centuries
back) where
secular and
sacred are all one.

Our most prized symbol is the walnut. The patio's walnut
tree we see
everyday from
a retreat many
would love for
themselves: a not
at all deep cut
that instantly scars
over in the bark of
the walnut tree
allows us to share
a glass of watered-
down black resin
(the resin that
Marina Tsvetaeva
dedicates to her
lover Sofia
Parnok): the
rest, knitting
singing, eating
fish cakes, taking a
walk (we have
to take the dog

nos llene los
aposentos de
cagarrutas y
pelotillas de lana
o algodón) (son
unos bestias estos
perros de peluche):
y así, llegar a casa,
despelotarnos ea,
despelotarnos y
ponernos a esperar
a la Puta muy puta
rezongona que
nunca llega en
pareja y que
dígase lo que
se diga siempre
somos nosotros
mismos, cada cual
en su hora y por
separado.

out we can't let it
fill our bedrooms
with dog poop
and spitballs
of wool and cotton)
(they're real beasts
these stuffed toy
dogs): and so, get
home, strip
off, strip off and
prepare ourselves
to wait for the
cranky bitchy Bitch
who never turns
up as a couple and
whatever anyone
says is always just
us, each in
our own time and
on our own.

Véase como después de esto a ésta ya no la vuelvo a ver

La salamandra, provista de la oscuridad
    sideral (mirad sus
    pupilas) se colocó
    a mi lado (a la
    izquierda) durante
    el desayuno, qué
    observaba: quede,
    especie de secreto,
    entre nosotros.
    ¿Qué comía
    mientras yo
    devoraba un
    desayuno
    suculento
    a la manera
    occidental? Aire
    suculento comía,
    moscas de aire,
    el residuo de la
    propia respiración
    de las moscas, los
    peces, las plantas
    deletéreas, el
    calostro negro
    de las madres.

Espanté a la salamandra que se volvió
    broche en el vestido
    floreado (amarillo,
    flores negras)
    (¿hortensias?)
    de mi mujer.

Sentimos por primera vez, más allá de las
    estrellas, más allá

Wherein it's seen how, once this is gone, I don't see it again

The salamander, possessed of the darkness of stars (look
    at its pupils) settled
    beside me (on my
    left) during
    breakfast, what
    was it observing:
    let it be, a kind
    of secret,
    between us.
    What was it eating
    while I was
    devouring a
    succulent
    Western-style
    breakfast?
    Succulent air,
    flies of air,
    it was eating
    the remnants of
    the flies' own
    breath, breath
    of fish, poisonous
    plants, the black
    colostrum of
    the mothers.

I shooed away the salamander that became the
    brooch on the
    floral dress (yellow,
    black flowers)
    (hydrangeas?)
    of my wife.

For the first time we felt, beyond the stars, beyond
    the retinue of

de la retahíla de
rituales (futesas)
que en todos
provoca el
pensamiento de
la Muerte, una
consternación:
ajena, claro está
a la orfandad. Sólo
la salamandra
tiene capacidad
de transformación.
Es el fuego y su
anterioridad. El
fuego y su
continuidad. Lo
incoado del fuego,
más allá de la
conflagración. Y
sólo la salamandra
(mirad, mirad sus
pupilas) aparece y
desaparece a mano
izquierda a la mesa,
por designio propio,
no es ángel mas
tampoco consulta
a Dios.

Y bien, ahí está Vega en nombre y en el
nombre de mi mujer:
a su lado, soy yo,
Deneb, que se
acerca a hurtadillas,
pies juntillas, el
eterno subrepticio,
el estrellado y

rituals (small talk)
that put together
summon the
thought of Death,
a sudden distress:
foreign, of course
to any orphan-
hood. Only
the salamander
has this capacity
for transformation.
It is fire and fire's
anteriority. Fire
and its continuity.
The unformed
nature of fire,
beyond conflagration.
And only the
salamander (look,
look at its pupils)
appears and
disappears on the
left-hand side at
the table, by its
own design, it's not
an angel nor does
it confer with
God.

Ah well, here is Vega by name, and in the name of
my wife: at her
side, it's
me, Deneb,
sneaking up close,
blindly, the eternal
stealthy one,
shattered and

desfondado por
miedos, y por
capas y capas de
consternación, el
estupefacto petrificado
en lo alto: en lo mollar
de las pupilas, en lo
resquebrajado. Sé
que miento al
encogerme de
hombros, simulo al
desentenderme de
mi muerte: salamandra,
mujer, al igual que
vosotras, tengo
miedo.

Sale el sol, viro la cara a Levante, junto las
manos y recito, los ojos
entrecerrados, sutras.
No permito durante
diez minutos ni una
sola obstrucción. A
eso al menos he
llegado, con base a
una práctica. Voy
poniendo la mesa,
servilleta doblada
de papel, cubiertos
de hojalata, el par
de platos redondos
o cuadrados, a veces
triangulares: y nos
sentamos herbívoros,
frugívoros, a un café,
un cacho de pan
tostado, tengo miedo

staved in by fears,
by layers and
layers of distress,
shocked, numbed,
turned to stone there
in the sky: in the
pupils' soft core,
in the crack. I know
I lie when I shrug
my shoulders, pretend
not to know about
my death: salamander,
woman, just like
you, I'm afraid.

The sun comes out, I turn my face to the East, join my hands and
recite sutras, my eyes
half closed. For ten
minutes I do not
allow even a single
distraction. At least
I've reached that
level, based on
practice. I go about
setting the table,
folded paper
serviette, tin
cutlery, two
round or square
plates, sometimes
triangular: and
we sit down
herbivores, frugivores,
to a coffee, a slice
of toast, I'm
frightened at not
being hungry: the

a no tener hambre:
brilla, cómo, el
mondadientes (el
agua) sobre la mesa,
el broche era de jade,
y de jade las dos
hormigas (residuos
titubeando de cornalina)
reconfigurando la
salamandra a mi lado
(izquierdo) de retirada,
hormiga tras hormiga
camino de la lucerna
(abierta, a propósito)
del techo del comedor.

toothpick (water)
on the table shines,
how? the brooch
was jade, and the
two ants both
jade (hesitant
remnants of carnelian)
reconfiguring the
salamander by my
(left) side in retreat,
ant after ant
towards the skylight
(open, on purpose) in
the dining room ceiling.

Véase como el convaleciente sienta la pauta de su propio final

El convaleciente sopesa el guijarro en la
     palma de la mano, de
     cobre viejo la Balanza
     del Juicio, el guijarro
     le quema los ojos: ésa
     es la piedra del sueño
     que lo hunde más
     abajo, lo perfora,
     gime la víscera
     ancestral, imposible
     reconocer la sustancia
     que guarda el origen,
     o no, de las secreciones:
     destino o no de la
     sustancia que lo
     aguarda, ni qué ni
     adónde: el guijarro
     le pesa en la palma
     de la mano, al fiel,
     en toda su blancura,
     una tonelada.

No se desvela porque en el fondo está
     muerto y ahora vive
     hacia arriba.

La ropa que se pone esta misma tarde
     se sobreentiende por
     omisión pertenece a
     la liturgia.

De ahí la música sacra que llega a sus
     oídos, no viene de
     lejos, mece la hierba

Wherein it is seen how the convalescent sets the pattern of his own ending

The convalescent feels the weight of the pebble in the palm of
    his hand, the Scales of
    Judgment made of
    old copper, the pebble
    burns his eyes: this is
    the dreamstone that
    sinks him most deeply,
    it perforates him, the
    ancestral entrails
    keen, impossible
    to ascertain the
    substance that preserves
    the origin, or not,
    of the secretions: fate
    or not of the substance
    that awaits it, neither
    why nor where: the
    pebble in the palm of
    his hand, on balance,
    in all its whiteness,
    weighs a ton.

He doesn't stay awake because he is essentially dead and
    now is living
    upwards.

The clothing he puts on this very afternoon
    belongs (it goes
    without saying)
    to the liturgy.

From there the sacred music reaching his ears, doesn't
    come from far
    away, it sways the

demasiado crecida
del patio, y la silla
de bambú, de alzarla
pesaría lo que el
hierro, las forjas
más inclementes,
los doce cimientos
de la ciudad
celeste, latente, la
madera sin tabular
(lo que duelen las
ortigas) del árbol del
origen.

Todo, a mano izquierda: por eso no se
     ladea, ahora comprende
     al idiota de mirada fija, la
     baba del que balbucea.

Una sola voz de cítara ceremonial, cuernos
     de caza para muertos,
     y el triple llamado
     intermitente del
     shofar: lo escucha
     mientras baja el
     primer viento noto
     de la montaña, le
     roza la cabeza
     tocada, está sin
     duda resguardado:
     por hoy amparado,
     limosna de la fusta,
     de la palma de la
     mano en el aire,
     al pie del Arca,
     de la mesa con
     la Balanza (panes
     ácimos) sopesando.

overgrown grass on
the patio, and the
bamboo chair, weighing
if you lift it the same
as iron, as the harshest
smithies, the twelve
foundations of the
celestial city, latent,
the untallied timber
(the nettles sting)
of the tree of
origin.

Everything, on the left: that's why he doesn't tip, now
he understands the
idiot with his fixed gaze,
the drool of his babblings.

A single voice from the ceremonial zither, hunting horns for
the dead, and the
intermittent triple
call of the *shofar*: he
hears it as the first
south wind comes
down from the mountain,
brushes his (ritually
covered) head, he's
protected for
sure: sheltered for
today, the whip's
charity, charity of the
palm of his hand in
the breeze, at the foot
of the Ark, of the
table with the Scale
(unleavened
loaves) weighing
it.

Véase como el durmiente constata las piezas que componen
al final el sueño

En

la etapa final sólo se sueña, lapsos con
       adormideras. Decúbito
       supino, el alimento
       imaginario, una sola
       voz (en mi caso de
       mujer) debajo: arriba
       (argollas; eslabones) su
       eco (concatenaciones).
       El contenido del sueño
       se puede describir en
       dos palabras. Tal y tal.
       Las imágenes, caseras.
       Un pájaro hornero
       termina su nido, brota
       la primera flor blanca
       del pomar, de golpe
       aparecen siete o
       nueve (qué más
       da) y de inmediato
       (progresión geométrica)
       cuaja el pomar. Flores
       blancas. Frutos rojos
       (verdes) nada más
       real. Islas (realismo)
       amarillas. Manos
       hechas a la recolección.
       Todas las canastas
       de mimbre reforzado.
       Todas las escaleras
       de aluminio (fácil
       alcanzar la copa
       del árbol). ¿Y aún el

Wherein it is seen how the sleeper verifies the elements that
in the end make up his dream

In

the last stage there's only dreaming, time spent among
poppies. Flat on
your back, fed on
imaginary food, a
single voice (in my
case a woman's) below:
above (rings; swivels) its
echo (links in a chain).
The dream's content
can be described in two
words. Such and such. The
images, domestic.
An ovenbird finishes
his nest, the first
white flower opens
in the apple orchard,
suddenly seven or
nine (whatever) appear
and immediately (a
geometric progression)
the orchard is full of
them. White
flowers. Red (green)
fruit nothing more
real. (Truly) yellow
islands. Hands made
for gathering. All the
wicker baskets
reinforced. All the
ladders in aluminum
(easy to reach the
tree's top). And the

sueño no se esfuma?
Dios, por ejemplo,
a ver: a intervalos,
entre nubes espesas
compuestas de vapor
(no son más que vapor)
(irrisorio su espesor).
Surge, se le escucha,
caramba, cuántos
idiomas sabe, ¿o será
que en la etapa final,
ciencia infusa, nos
posee el conocimiento
del idioma anterior a
Babel? Abel. Ése sí
que la pasó mal.
Pasar las de Abel, he
ahí la verdad al final.
Sueña Abel Babel,
llega Caín, quijada
de burro en mano,
y conmina a sentarse
a comer cabrito (Abel
quiere malanga).
¿Triunfará la paz
universal? Y donde
el sueño se empieza
a deshilvanar, blanca
hilacha, oquedad
sideral, se planta
Dios al pie del Trono,
acompasada visión
muestra al durmiente,
sonámbulo lirón, unos
ramilletes blancos,
unos troncos retorcidos,
canastas atestadas,

dream still hasn't
vanished? To see
God, for example: now
and then, between thick
clouds made of vapor
(they're nothing but vapor)
(ridiculously thick). He
appears, they listen to
him, what the hell, how
many languages does
he know, or in our last
phase, through some
innate knowledge, will we
have understanding of the
language before Babel?
Abel. For him no doubt
about it things went very
bad, a real hell. To live
Abel's fate, that's the
truth in the end. Abel
dreams Babel, Cain
turns up, a donkey's
jawbone in his hand,
threatening to sit
down and eat a kid goat
(Abel prefers taro). Will
universal peace triumph?
And where the dream's
thread begins to unravel,
white thread, a great
hole among the stars, God
stands firm at the foot of
the Throne, vision slowly
adjusting reveals to the
dreamer, a sleepwalker in
a deep trance, white clusters
of flowers, a few gnarled

primer mordisco,
primer gusano en la
carne, algo ácida,
algo seca, de la

manzana.

trunks, laden baskets,
first bite, first worm in
the apple's, slightly
acidic, slightly dry,

flesh.

Véase como el soñador descubre que el suyo es el mejor de los mundos posibles

Sigo a propósito dormido, cante el gallo
　　cuando le dé la
　　gana, su cresta
　　violeta incrustada
　　en mi sueño, me
　　niego a despertar:
　　ya no concibo el
　　amanecer.

Un poco de crema en la avena, unos
　　buches de café, el
　　sátiro barrigudo
　　perdió las pezuñas,
　　salta por mí de la
　　cama: atiende a
　　las necesidades de
　　la ablución, pasar la
　　lengua por las motas
　　de polvo en el rayo
　　de sol que penetra
　　por la ventana
　　(entreabierta) está
　　atareado: no me
　　entrometo, no
　　me inmuto, sigo
　　durmiendo, a carta
　　cabal me dejo
　　desnudar, zarandear,
　　parezco un monigote
　　al que lavan, entalcan,
　　perfuman, y sólo lo
　　arropan de blanco, el
　　blanco de los ojos y
　　el blanco almidonado

Wherein it is seen how the dreamer discovers that his is the best of all possible worlds

I deliberately go on sleeping, let the rooster sing when it
    feels like it,
    its violet crest
    encrusted in
    my dream, I
    refuse to wake up:
    I can't imagine
    dawn anymore.

A little cream on the oats, a few mouthfuls of coffee, the
    potbellied satyr's
    lost his hooves, on my
    behalf he leaps out
    of bed: attends to the
    necessities of
    ablution, runs his
    tongue along the
    motes of dust in
    the sun's ray that
    enters through the
    (half open) window
    he's busy: I don't
    interfere, don't bat
    an eyelid, stay sleeping,
    surrendering completely
    let myself be undressed,
    flipped around, I'm like a
    rag doll they wash, dust
    with talcum powder,
    perfume, and they're
    wrapping the doll only
    in white, the white of
    the eyes and the
    starched (passive)

(inactivo) de las
mortajas: la nueva
vestimenta (chillona)
del gallo encaramado
a la cerca, a un metro
del sátiro, el sátiro
mea, el gallo lo
embarra, y yo río
a mandíbula batiente
agarrado a la baranda
de la cama de hierro.

Y así va el día por allá afuera. Yo me
desentiendo. Los
calcetines sucios,
sicote: se le podrá
exprimir todavía
esa gota de tinta
violeta que se
empoza: viruta
la gota que se
empoza, tarugo
la nariz afilada.
Y lo voy a escribir,
baldado, el cuarto
al amanecer
cercenado por el
sueño. Me arrebujo.
Y lo traigo de fuera,
mi mejor recuerdo,
el señero, sea vidrio
o sea madera, me
da lo mismo: porque
es concreto: en
Feldafing: luego de
la siesta y mi segundo
ataque de pánico de

white of shrouds: the
new (bright red)
vestments of the
rooster perched on
the fence, one meter
from the satyr, the satyr
urinates, the rooster
covers him with muck,
and I laugh my head off
holding on to the rail
of the iron bed.

And so the day goes by out there. I wash my hands of it.
 Dirty socks, foot
odor: you can
still squeeze out
the drop of violet
ink that pools
there: wood shavings
the drop forming a
puddle, my pointy nose
a door stopper.
I'm going to write it,
hobbled, the room
at dawn cut short
by sleep. I wrap myself
up. I bring in from
outside my best
memory, unique,
glass or wood, it's the
same to me: because
it's concrete: in
Feldafing: after
siesta and my second
panic attack in
February, stretching wide,
the lake in the background,

febrero, desperezados,
el lago al fondo, aquel
día ni lo miramos. Me
fui a pasear de su
cintura, por esa fecha
comenzaron mis
temblores, desparpajo
en la mirada de ambos:
en el bosque de los
pinos mansos nos
sentamos a fumar
(nosotros que jamás
fumamos) a callar
(nosotros que nunca
dejábamos de conversar).
Había que verlo, aquello,
las sibilas, Diana y las
tres ocas, el viejo del
gabán raído (pero eso
era pura fantasmagoría)
y lo mejor, las cornejas
en celo bailando, era
para no despertar.

that day we didn't even
look at it. I left to take a
walk my arm around her
waist, on that date my
tremors began, chutzpah
in both our
eyes: in the forest of
umbrella pines we sat
and smoked (we who
never smoke) fell
silent (we who never
stop conversing).
You had to see it, that
thing, the sibyls, Diana
and the three white
geese, the old man
with his threadbare
overcoat (a pure
fantasy on my part)
and best of all, the jackdaws
about to mate and
dancing, if only I didn't
have to wake up.

Véase como en el tránsito nos vemos sometidos todavía a los pensamientos

Me dejo llevar, allá otros bordes, aguas
    verdosas (subterráneas):
    he soterrado durante
    años unas (pocas)
    ideas, mil y un
    denuestos, nadie
    me escuchó, ni
    nadie oyó de mi
    boca, reniegos. Y
    aquí me maldigo
    hoy por pusilánime.

La barca a la deriva, pinaza repintada antes
    de zarpar, curioso los
    viejos gustamos de la
    intensidad del rojo: a
    la manera china, rojos
    y dorados. Di dos
    manos de pintura a
    la pinaza, no me dio
    tiempo de lavarme
    las manos con
    aguarrás: apenas
    me pude ataviar
    para el recorrido:
    bombachos y blusón
    colorados, casquete
    negro de seda,
    zapatillas rosadas
    de esparto, mis
    ancestros se van
    a creer que me
    volví maricón.

Wherein it is seen how even in the transit we are prey to thoughts

I surrender to the journey, over there different frontiers, greenish
    (subterranean) waters:
    for years I've kept buried
    some (a few)
    ideas, a thousand
    and one insults, no one
    listened to me, and no
    one heard cuss words
    from my lips. And now
    I curse myself for being
    a coward.

The boat drifting, a pinnace repainted before setting sail,
    curious how we old
    men enjoy the
    intensity of red: in
    Chinese style, reds
    and golds. I gave the
    pinnace two coats
    of paint, there
    was no time
    to wash my hands
    with turpentine: I
    barely had
    a moment to
    dress for the trip:
    red baggy pants and
    peasant shirt, black
    silk cap, pink
    hemp sandals, my
    ancestors are going
    to think I've turned
    into a faggot.

Aguas tardas, predestinadas. ¿será posible que
     aquí debajo llueva, y no
     sea azufre, pedrisco
     ígneo?¿Quién vive?
     ¿Cómo coño quién
     vive si aquí somos
     un hatajo de muertos?
     Irreprimibles. Oídnos
     cantar más que cuitas,
     sandeces. Y blasfemias.
     Y amorosas lucubraciones,
     rimas jocosas donde impera
     la lubricidad.

En un rato, al otro borde, les haré un corte de
     manga a mis antepasados.
     Y si Dios existe caeré de
     hinojos, la mano derecha
     extendida, las manchas
     de pintura roja por
     seguro revelan mis
     ocultos vituperios:
     irán apareciendo
     quienes denosté,
     protesto, se lo tenían
     merecido. La ofrenda
     en la mano extendida,
     rápido, Señor, que se
     me cansa. ¿Sí o no?
     Una campanilla imita
     gorjeos plateados,
     ofrezco un jabón de
     olor a base de glicerina,
     lo que me queda del
     sándwich.

Late, predestined waters. Is it possibly going to rain here
    below, rain not
    brimstone, a fiery
    hail? Who's there?
    How the hell can anyone
    be here if we're a
    bunch of stiffs? An
    irrepressible bunch. Listen
    as, instead of love's
    sorrows, we sing bits of
    nonsense. And blasphemies.
    And amorous fantasies,
    joking rhymes where
    lewdness dominates.

In a moment, on the other shore, I'll give the finger to my
    ancestors. And if God
    exists I'll fall to
    my knees, my right
    hand stretched
    out, the stains of
    red paint showing
    quite clearly my hidden
    offences: they'll keep
    on appearing, all those
    I reviled, I protest,
    they deserved it.
    The offering in my
    outstretched hand, take
    it quickly, Lord, my
    hand's tired. Yes or no?
    A hand bell mimics
    silvery chirping, I offer a
    fragrant soap made from
    glycerin, what remains of
    my sandwich.

Véase como la muerte se desdobla en una mariposa de luz

Me alejé. Los nervios, alterados. Sentado en
   el suelo de la sala,
   ella acude a mi
   mente, bozal: está
   muy desmejorada.
   Acude él, impertérrito,
   carlanca.

Un solo mueble. A unos metros de distancia
   revolotea una
   mariposa de luz,
   bozal y carlanca
   a la mirada, no
   quiero presenciar
   los revoloteos del
   bicho ese que
   exasperan al más
   pintado, hiérase
   contra la pared,
   llaga se haga
   contra un bombillo
   aún prendido,
   polvillo en un
   rayo de luz la
   mariposa.

De lejos, todo de lejos. Inmovilidad. Imaginarme
   esfera fija en el
   firmamento, estrella
   por ejemplo inamovible,
   negro agujero
   (adentro) del bicho,
   hora de quitarme
   de un solo tirón
   la ropa (cerúlea)

Wherein it is seen how death opens out in a moth

I moved away. My nerves, agitated. Sitting on the living room
    floor, she comes into my
    mind, muzzle: she's not
    looking at all well.
    He comes into my mind,
    with no sense of fear,
    a halter.

A single piece of furniture. A few meters away a moth
    spins, muzzle and
    dog collar visible,
    I don't want to
    witness the bug's
    weaving circles
    that drive the
    most patient
    crazy, let it
    crash against a
    wall, do itself
    harm on a still
    burning light bulb,
    the moth
    dust specks in
    a ray of light.

From far off, everything from far off. Motionlessness. To imagine
    myself an unmoving sphere
    in the firmament, a
    fixed star for
    example, a black
    hole inside the
    bug, time with a
    single jerk to
    take off the
    (sky blue) clothing

que visto hace
semanas: quedarme
quieto (Bodhidarma)
ante la pared, ante
el bombillo.

La mariposa de luz cayó al suelo, boca arriba
por supuesto, a unos
metros de distancia
soplé, soplé otra vez,
el rastro de su polvo.
Puede que fuese
lepisma, efímera,
mantis religiosa
no: son los primeros
datos de la conciencia
con que me identifico
esta mañana.

Lejísimos. Se trata de un desván con vista a
un placer, cascajos,
yerbazal, una mula
más vieja que la
mula de Matusalén.
Mataduras (desolladuras)
crece lampazo, crece
la pamplina. Me pongo
de pie, taparrabo
y túnica carmelita
(carmelitosa). Miro
cascajo. Y al rato
tomo la irrefutable
decisión de imaginar
los escenarios
naturales (están en
Suiza) más bellos
de que soy capaz.

I've worn for weeks:
to stay silent
(Bodhidharma)
before the wall, before
the light bulb.

The moth fell to the floor, on its back of course, a few meters
    from it I blew away
    once, then twice
    the traces of its
    dust. Possibly it
    might have been a
    silverfish, a mayfly,
    not a praying
    mantis: those
    are the first data of
    consciousness
    I identify with
    this morning.

Very far away. I'm in an attic with views of a vacant lot,
    piles of rubble, patches of
    weeds, a mule older than
    the mule of Methuselah.
    Sores (grazes) burdock
    is flourishing, chickweed
    is flourishing. I stand up,
    loin cloth and brown
    (brownish) tunic. I'm
    looking at rubble. And
    right then I take
    the inescapable
    decision to imagine
    the most beautiful
    scenes from nature
    (they're in
    Switzerland) I'm
    able to.

De común acuerdo salimos a pasear. Es la hora
	del día cuando todo
	se rectifica, concuerda,
	con naturalidad: los
	recodos del camino,
	y esto salta a la vista,
	se vuelven línea recta,
	la más recta línea
	concebible: un asunto
	entre dos. Ejemplos:
	entre ella y él que
	me legaron bozal y
	carlanca; entre mi
	amada y yo a la hora
	del paseo, al llegar
	a la orilla del lago
	(recordad que
	estamos en Suiza,
	país considerado)
	nos hundimos; entre
	mi sombra y yo,
	triunfo del gallo
	que anuncia la
	disolución de la
	carne en la sombra,
	de la sombra en el
	polvillo de la mariposa
	que anoche se estrelló
	contra el bombillo al
	apagar la luz. ¿Yo?

Llegué al Paraíso, cogí turno, y entré. Dogal, bozal,
	carlanca, me pongo
	a silbar. Y como el
	Trono está vacío,
	trepo; y como la
	mariposa de luz da

By mutual consent we go out and have a walk. It's the hour of
     day when everything
     adjusts naturally, finds
     mutual concord: the
     bends of the road, this
     is at once absolutely
     clear, turn into a
     straight line, the
     straightest line
     imaginable: a personal
     matter between two
     people. Examples:
     between the two of them
     who bequeathed me
     muzzle and halter;
     between my beloved
     and me at the time
     of our walk, on
     reaching the lakeshore
     (remember we're in
     Switzerland, a renowned
     country) we collapse;
     between my shadow and
     myself, the rooster's
     triumph announces the
     dissolution of the flesh in
     darkness, of darkness
     (dissolving) in the moth's
     dust where last night it
     exploded against the
     light bulb so that too
     was extinguished.
     Was it me?

I've reached Paradise, waited my turn and entered. Halter,
     muzzle, dog collar, I
     start to whistle. And

vueltas en redondo
a la entrada del ano
de la mula, cascajo
(miro) yerbazal
(miro, de lejos):
tengo por primera
vez la convicción
absoluta (inescrutable)
de haber estado a la
puerta (la vi, la vi
revolotear) de la
sala.

since the Throne is
empty, I climb
up; and as the
moth spins around
the entrance of the
mule's anus, (I'm
seeing) rubble (from
far away I see) weeds:
for the first time I
have the absolute
(inexplicable) conviction
of having been at
(I saw it, I saw it
spinning) the door of
the living room.

Véase como una joven no tan joven se pone
a esperar amores

Desanimada
a izquierda a derecha se mira (la mira) en
        el espejo del botiquín
        (de arriba abajo) esa
        cara de todos los días,
        ese bonete medieval,
        el encaje del cuello de
        la blusa, esos pechos
        deprimidos, reducidos
        a su más mínima
        expresión.

    Y
luego nadie a la puerta, un rostro detrás de
        su rostro, al menos
        un insecto detenido
        en un punto (detrás)
        de la pared: acercaría
        la yema del dedo, lo
        rozaría llamándolo
        al oído escarabajo,
        animalillo, negrura
        y redondez de Dios,
        o lo que se le ocurriera.

    Besar
su costra. El pie zopo parece que tiene cura,
        hoy día hay manera
        de aumentar el grosor
        de los pechos, cuánto
        no podría remediarse
        acudiendo a la cirugía,
        salir del quirófano
        remozada, un vestido

Wherein it's seen how a young but not so young woman gets ready to wait for lovers

Losing heart
from left to right she looks at herself in the mirror of
    the medicine cabinet
    (looks at) (from top to
    bottom) that everyday
    face, that medieval
    headgear, the lace trim
    on the collar of her
    blouse, those sunken
    breasts, reduced to
    their minimal
    expression.

And
then no one at the door, a face behind her face, apart from
    an insect frozen
    in one spot (behind)
    the wall: her finger
    tip might reach it,
    might graze it and softly
    name it scarab beetle,
    tiny creature, God's
    round black shell, or
    whatever strikes her.

To kiss
its crust. Her maimed foot apparently curable, today there's
    a way to increase the
    size of the breasts, what
    can't be fixed with the
    help of surgery, come
    out of the operating
    room with a new
    younger look, a

floreado, unos
ajustadores negros
de puntilla (de putilla)
se ríe ahora delante
del espejo.

Se
pondría te digo (se dice) (le dice a la del
    espejo, a la desanimada)
    a bailar: la jiga, un minué,
    y en su versión (visión)
    putilla, un cancán.
    Se le vean al vuelo
    las piernas. Rodillas
    redondas. Corvas
    abiertas (sumisas).
    La altura más cercana
    al entronque del muslo
    con la ingle, el mocho
    de vello negro de sus
    pudendas que reluciera,
    cuánto ha, a sus diez
    años de edad.

Está
todo pendiente (de un hilo) (de meterle mano
    a sus ahorros) (de que
    le metan cuchilla a la
    deformación congénita)
    (gracias, mamá):
    silicona, flor de tela,
    escote amplio, aumentar
    lo justo de peso (método
    científico): sentarse, y
    de buen ánimo, por
    Dios, de buen ánimo,
    a esperar al que está,

floral dress, black
lace (sexy call girl)
bra she's laughing
now before the
mirror.

She's
maybe getting ready I tell you (she tells herself) (tells her self in
    the mirror, the one
    who's lost heart) to
    dance: the gigue, a minuet,
    and in its sexy call girl
    version (vision) a
    cancan. Her legs on
    display as she spins.
    Rounded knees. The back
    of her knees open
    (submissive). The
    height closest to
    where the thigh meets
    the groin, the cropped
    black fuzz of her
    pudenda that maybe
    first glistened, how long
    ago is it now, when she
    was ten.

It's
all hanging (from a thread) (to get their hands on her
    savings) (they might
    take a scalpel to her
    congenital deformation)
    (thanks mom): silicon,
    floral fabric, ample
    neckline, to gain the
    necessary weight (by
    scientific method): to sit,

sombra de sombras,
detrás de la puerta:
la puerta se abrirá,
rechinando, abierta
se oirán dos pasos,
justo dos pasos, se
abrirá otra puerta
(¿igual de alta?)
(¿igual de gruesa?)
dos pasos, otra
puerta: ella mira,
y mira (la mira) en
el espejo del botiquín
desde la silla de
tijera en medio de la
sala (vacía) la puerta
se abrirá de par en
par, luz, más luz,
mucha luz, relumbre,
deslumbramiento del
escarabajo que inicia
su descenso en la

pared.

and with a cheerful mind, by
God a cheerful mind, to
wait for what's there, the
shadow of all shadows,
behind the door: the door
will slowly squeak open,
once opened, two audible
steps, exactly two steps,
another door will open (the
same height?) (equal
thickness?) two steps,
another door: she looks, and
from the folding chair at
the center of the (empty)
lounge room sees (sees it)
in the medicine cabinet
mirror the door will open
wide, light, more light, much
light, shining light, the
dazzling glare of the scarab
beetle beginning its
descent down the

wall.

Véase como unos metros de tierra colorada contribuyen al orden

La cosecha no fue mala, que un traspatio
    produzca suficiente
    para el resto del año,
    y no, no estamos en
    diciembre, y quede
    aún espacio para
    cultivar flores de
    ornamento, la cala
    en particular, es de
    agradecer.

Lo agradezco a la azada, al escardador, la
    boñiga del caballo,
    la plasta de vaca,
    el fuego interior
    que me anima a
    mis sesenta años
    a sembrar en el
    traspatio de esta
    casa (al límite)
    hortalizas, legumbres,
    yerbas medicinales:
    una reverencia sobre
    todo a la lombriz de
    tierra y al cocuyo
    que de noche
    ilumina mis pupilas,
    mis rastreos al paso
    de su pirotecnia, el
    bicho me centra.

La Eternidad no existe, existe la cebolla.

Wherein it is seen how a few meters of red soil contribute to order

The harvest wasn't bad, that a backyard should produce enough
    for the rest of the year,
    and no, it's not
    December, and there's
    still maybe space
    to cultivate ornamental
    flowers, the calla
    lily in particular, is
    something to be
    grateful for.

I give thanks to the hoe, the weeder, the horse dung, the
    cow manure, the
    inner passion that
    drives me at
    sixty years of
    age to sow in the
    backyard of
    this house (to
    maximum capacity)
    vegetables, legumes,
    medicinal herbs:
    above all a bow
    of thanks to the
    earthworm and the
    firefly that by night
    illuminates the pupils
    of my eyes, my groping
    searches, by means of
    its pyrotechnics, the
    bug centers me.

Eternity does not exist, the onion exists.

Tegumentos,
capas,
lloriqueo
nasal
y
ocular,
el
cuchillo,
la
madre,
el
delantal
y
un
chisporroteo
cardinal,
alquimia

continua de la semilla que regresa a la
        tierra removida, por
        mí, por mí, sesenta
        años y animoso, voy
        del traspatio al suelo
        por la cotidiana vía
        matutina (ciego colon
        duodeno íleon) (ano)
        de la deposición.

Bravo mojón a la conformación de la vaina
        atiborrada de
        guisantes.

Bravos guisantes la boca atiborrando a la
        hora del almuerzo
        deviniendo tras
        birlibirloques de
        Dios, mojón a la
        mañana.

Seedpods,
layers,
tears
from
nose
and
eyes,
the
knife,
the
mother,
the
apron
and
a
primordial
crackling,
alchemy

of the seed continues as it goes back to the soil churned up
    by me, by me,
    sixty years old and
    full of life, I go to the
    backyard soil by the
    daily morning
    route (cecum colon
    duodenum ileum)
    (anus) of defecation.

Wondrous turd before the structure of the pod crammed
    full with peas.

Wondrous peas the mouth crammed at lunch time
    becoming
    through God's
    magic the
    morning turd.

Qué vaina. Cuánto rigor. Cuánta dirección,
    magnitud. Y allá
    arriba la veleta
    dando las horas
    alrededor de
    un eje, cuatro
    estaciones,
    cuatro puntos
    cardinales, y
    cuatro comensales
    a papa por cabeza
    (la boca está en la
    cabeza, la lombriz
    aireando la tierra
    roja del traspatio,
    el Orbe en orden).

Me siento, regüeldo (Sancho, has de decir
    eructo que no regüeldo)
    viene noche, llega
    sueño, hago caso
    y me adormezco:
    sumido desciendo en
    la semilla (cotiledón;
    embrión) ya pronto
    resplandezco novia
    de blanco en el
    cantero al fondo
    del traspatio, de

malvas
criadero.

What a pain of a pea pod. So much precision. So much direction,
  greatness. And there
  up above the
  weathercock
  announcing the
  time around its
  axis, four seasons,
  four cardinal
  points, and four
  diners at the table
  one potato per head
  (the mouth is in the
  head, the earthworm
  oxygenating the red
  soil of the backyard, the
  globe in order).

I sit down, I burp (Sancho, you must say belch not
  burp) night
  comes, sleep
  comes, I pay heed
  and nod off: immersed
  I go down into
  the seed (cotyledon;
  embryo) straight
  away I am shining
  a bride in white in
  the flowerbed at the
  bottom of the backyard, a

nursery
of
daisies.

Véase como, como dice el refrán, nunca es tarde
si la dicha, etc.

En su habla empezaron a aparecer solecismos,
      máculas en la ortografía:
      del reverso de las
      palabras surgían a
      chorros funciones
      ininteligibles.

¿Se daba cuenta? Por vez primera en su vida
      escribió poesía, a
      chorros: todo en
      su pupila de repente
      reverberaba. Oía
      caer una moneda
      en el suelo de tablas,
      salía disparado en
      diagonal un pájaro.
      El pájaro se volvía
      alcotán. El alcotán
      Aldebarán, brazos
      en jarras se ponía
      a brincar en la
      pequeña habitación
      trastera que ahora
      denominaba gabinete
      de trabajo.

El amanuense, y no es que hubiera amasado
      una fortuna, dejó
      su empleo de años,
      una módica pensión,
      unos ahorros, y la
      costumbre de no
      incurrir en gastos
      más allá de la
      alimentación,
      el gato, de vez

Wherein it is seen how, as the saying goes,
if something is great it's worth the . . .

Solecisms began to turn up in his speech, blotches in his
        handwriting: from the
        reverse side of words
        an abundance of
        unintelligible functions
        appeared.

Did he realize? For the first time in his life he wrote
        poetry, tons of it:
        suddenly everything
        in the pupils of his eyes
        was shimmering. He
        could hear a coin
        drop on the wooden
        floor, in a flash a
        bird would dart away
        diagonally. The bird
        became a falcon. The
        falcon Aldebaran, his
        arms at his waist, he
        started jumping
        up and down in the
        small backroom
        he now called the
        work office.

An amanuensis, and it's not that he'd amassed a
        fortune, he left his
        job of many years,
        a modest pension, a
        few savings, and the
        habit of not incurring
        expenses beyond
        food, the cat, from
        time to time a

en cuando un
pantalón o una
camisa floreada
(era ahora poeta)
le facilitaron esta
nueva existencia
radiante (irradiante)
donde vislumbraba,
si no todo el tiempo,
al menos varias veces
a la semana, prímulas,
dunas, cimitarras, a la
salida del cuarto: y
jóvenes gaditanas
bailando en ánforas
de cerámica roja,
jóvenes de negro,
al pecho el camafeo
de las madres, las
rubias trenzas de
las campesinas
rusas de antes de
la Revolución (la
poesía enseña que
hay cosas que no
cambian, cuerpos
inmutables, tapices
ancestrales que
desconocen la
imperfección).

El acebo, craso, lustroso. Las almadías rumbo
a deltas innombrables.
El loto de la nieve en
las alturas japonesas,
tibetanas, nieves
perpetuas, lotos
sacramentales. La
basta comida, papa,

pair of trousers or
floral shirt (he was
a poet now) they eased
this new radiant
(radiating) existence
where he glimpsed, if
not all the time at
least several times a
week, primroses, sand
dunes, scimitars, as he
left the room: and
young women of Cadiz
dancing on red
ceramic amphorae,
young men in black,
cameos of their mothers
above their hearts, blonde
braids of Russian
peasant girls from
before the Revolution
(poetry teaches there
are things that don't
change, ageless
bodies, ancestral
tapestries alien to all
imperfection).

Holly, succulent, glossy. Rafts
heading towards
unnameable deltas.
The snow lotus
on Japanese, Tibetan
heights, perpetual
snows, sacramental
lotus flowers. Basic
plain food, potatoes,
buckwheat, barley,
carrots, a sweet. The
chipped plate, Sèvres,

alforfón, cebada,
zanahoria, manjar.
El plato descantillado,
Sèvres, por así decir.
Predicados alterados.
Divertido eso de
trasponer elementos
que configuran las
oraciones. Tremendas
palabras son hipérbaton,
perífrasis, enclítico. Oh
la la, catacresis. Y Oh
la la, sinécdoque.

Paul Klee. Satie. Cuánta cosa. Y el tipo ese que
escribe poemas cortos,
treinta y una sílabas,
y luego, medio mundo
se pasa siglos, vaya
cosa, estudiándolos.
Se puso de nombre
Plátano Estéril, hay
que ver. El amanuense,
sesenta años cumplidos,
despierta al rayar el
alba, té, aguas menores,
acoge en el cuaderno
(tapas duras) alcores,
regatos, rediles, no ve
nada, nada nunca en
absoluto (caray, ni en
relativo): impresionante
sin embargo el número
crujiente de páginas
atestadas en el número
creciente de cuadernos
acumulados sobre el
camastro de pino
(blanco).

more or less. Transposed
predicates. An amusing
business transposing the
elements that form
sentences. Hyperbaton,
periphrasis, enclitic are
awesome words. Ooh la la,
catachresis. And ooh la la,
synecdoche.

Paul Klee. Satie. Amazing things. And the guy who
    writes short poems,
    thirty-one syllables,
    and next, half the world
    spends centuries, can you
    believe it, studying them.
    He took the name Sterile
    Banana Tree, incredible. The
    amanuensis, aged
    sixty, wakes at dawn,
    drinks tea, passes water,
    in his notebook (sturdy
    covers) embraces hills,
    small channels of water,
    sheepfolds, he sees
    nothing, nothing
    ever absolutely
    (damn it, not even
    relatively): all the same
    it's impressive the
    staggering number of
    pages crammed in the
    growing number of
    notebooks piled up
    on the rickety old
    (white) pine
    bed.

Véase con qué sencillez se puede vivir en ciertos lugares

Acá

la temperatura es intermedia, se ajusta a
    la piel, no sobresalta
    la mente, fluctúa
    poco, una humedad
    media, amanece y
    anochece de golpe,
    las habitaciones
    resplandecen, luz
    invariable, dieciséis
    horas: por el reloj.

Quienes

leen (y acá todos leemos) dependemos de la
    luz natural, candiles,
    lámparas de aceite,
    la práctica de las
    devociones las
    hacemos en
    lamparillas donde
    chisporrotea la
    mantequilla, se
    llaman mariposas.
    Un atrio amplio,
    unos cuantos
    devotos, el gato
    adormilado, taja
    la luz la noche
    y nos ponemos
    a cantar.

Desacompasados.

Wherein it is seen how simply one can live in certain places

Here

the temperature is midrange, it adjusts to your skin, it
    doesn't jar your
    mind, fluctuates
    only slightly, the
    humidity moderate,
    the sun rises and sets
    instantaneously, the
    rooms dazzle,
    unchanging
    light, for sixteen
    hours: by the clock.

For whoever

reads (and here we all read) we rely on natural light,
    candles, oil
    lamps, we practice
    our devotions
    using small lamps
    where butter
    sizzles, we call
    them butterflies.
    A wide atrium, a
    few devotees, the
    cat dozing, light
    cuts the darkness
    and we start
    to sing.

All out of rhythm.

Which bugged me, months ago I decided to go out at night and

A qué me dio hace meses por salir a pescar de
            noche. Una camiseta
            a rayas que la luna
            raya (riela) su cabrilleo
            en la tela, tela desteñida,
            me hace sentir como si
            fuera un dios. Menor.
            Un dios derrotado. Lo
            que agradezco a los
            dioses. Y veo saltar
            peces cuyos nombres
            desconozco desde
            pequeño: les doy
            nombre tipo Neptuno,
            Afrodita, Juno, Ares,
            a los feos denomino
            Perséfone, a los
            gordos Ceres. Y
            sentado en el bote
            río.

Cicuta

le diera al mundo para que me dejen solo. El
            jamo de seda natural,
            estampado (lotos y
            cormoranes). La
            plomada doble, el
            flotador pintado de
            rojo. El anzuelo
            doble (tengo toda
            una colección
            ordenada por
            tamaño, hecha a
            mano: mis manos:
            estas manos
            artríticas, hechas
            sólo a leer). Sentado,

fish. A striped T-shirt
the moon marks
(shimmers) its
glittering stripes on the
fabric, faded fabric,
making me feel as if I
were a god. A minor god.
A vanquished one. For
which I give thanks
to the gods. And I see
fish leaping whose
names I haven't known
since childhood: I give
them a name like
Neptune, Aphrodite, Juno,
Ares, the ugly ones I
call Persephone, the fat
ones Ceres. And
sitting in the boat
I laugh.

I'd

give the world hemlock so they'd leave me alone. The
        net of natural silk,
        decorated (lotuses
        and cormorants). The
        double sinker, the
        float painted red.
        The double hook
        (I have a whole
        collection arranged
        by size, handmade:
        my hands: these
        arthritic hands,
        made only for
        reading). Sitting,

la carnada ajustada,
lanzo la pita, de
inmediato me siento
deseoso, impaciencia
de que piquen, piquen
ya.

En

somnolencia me voy adentrando en las grutas,
negros arrecifes,
anémonas amarillas
de mar, las crecientes,
los remolinos, las
devastadoras
inundaciones, y la
nieve, cellisca y
aguanieve, y las
tierras heladas
donde el río
desemboca en
una rada oscura.
Noche perpetua.
Un bote encallado.
No es el mío. Esto
lo tengo por seguro.
Sus remos son de
hierro color cardenillo,
su quilla de quebracho,
y sobre el hombro del
botero (no quisiera
exagerar pero es
bicéfalo) la lechuza
enamorada amamanta
a la rabiche, paloma
de paz, paloma del

cese.

the bait fixed, I
throw the line,
immediately I'm
all eagerness,
impatient for them
to bite, bite
now.

Half

asleep I drift deeper and deeper into the caverns, dark
　　reefs, yellow sea
　　anemones, tidal
　　surges, whirlpools,
　　catastrophic deluges,
　　snow, sleet, and
　　icy slush, and the
　　frozen lands where
　　the river flows out
　　into a dark inlet.
　　Perpetual night.
　　A boat that's
　　run aground.
　　It's not mine. I'm
　　sure of that. Its oars
　　are verdigris-colored
　　iron, its keel
　　quebracho
　　wood, and on the
　　boatman's shoulder
　　(I don't want to
　　exaggerate but he's
　　two headed) an owl
　　in love suckles
　　a laurel pigeon, the
　　dove of peace, dove of

truce.

Véase en que estado de sobreexcitación se encuentra el tiempo

En
estos
días

el reloj está haciendo de las suyas, y no es el
    mecanismo: ajusté
    las ruedas dentadas,
    me desnudé,
    trasvasé agua a
    arena, y viceversa:
    sol a sombra, y
    sin embargo, el
    reloj de pared se
    desordena por los
    techos, el suelo,
    las manecillas
    desarreglan en
    estos días el orden
    aritmético, estoy
    ido (estoy viejo):
    la disimilitud, el
    horario puesto
    de cabeza, me

consternan.
El número astral una pantomima. La base
    pitagórica del Universo
    otra ficción de la
    original imperfección
    (no hay poética que
    la subsane): lo poco
    que aclara la mística
    numeración no pasa
    de ser un fingimiento

Wherein time is seen getting overexcited

These
days

time is doing its own thing, and it's not the mechanism,
I adjusted
the cogwheels,
undressed,
transferred water to
sand, and vice versa:
sun to shade, and all
the same the wall
clock is thrown into
chaos by the
ceilings, the floor,
its hands these
days disrupt
the arithmetic
order, I'm dumb-
founded (I'm old):
unfamiliar things, time
turned upside down,
dismay

me.
The astral number a pantomime. The Pythagorean foundation of
the Universe one
more fiction for the
original imperfection
(there's no poetics to
offset it): the little
that throws light
on the mystic
numbers doesn't get
beyond being (yet another)
hocus-pocus.

(más). Finge la Muerte
una Nada y la Nada
finge una Presencia
donde no cabe nada.
Y cabe la Nada,
lueñe, lueñe, me
encuentro yo, veo
el mismo reloj de
siempre (en la
pulsera, sobre
el velador, en la
araña que teje,
en la flagrante
enumeración de
lo aparente): del
uno al doce,
romano, árabe,
sombra de
cifras, sílabas
balbucientes. En
el carillón, coronas,
resortes, la

tracción
del tiempo haciendo desde hace días de las
       suyas, trasvasa y
       trasvasa de los
       péndulos a las
       campanillas
       (alarmas) el
       mecanismo sin
       duda se ha zafado,
       veo motas, copos,
       ascuas intermitentes:
       en un reloj de agua,
       el

Death feigns
a Nothing and Nothingness
feigns a Presence where
nothing fits. And close by
Nothingness, a
long, long way off, I find
myself, I see the same
old clock (in the
wristwatch, on the
bedside table, in
the spider's
spinning, in
the blatant
enumeration of the
obvious): from numbers
one to twelve, Roman,
Arabic, ghost
numbers, stuttering
syllables. In the
carillon, the winders,
the springs, the

traction
of time doing its own thing for days, transferring
and transferring
from pendulums to
bells (alarms)
the mechanism
has no doubt about
it got out of joint,
I see specks,
balls of fluff,
occasional
embers: in a water
clock,

desmoronamiento.
De la estrella que guía, de la mano rugosa que
    ampara, de la tierna
    mirada momentánea
    en los vislumbres de
    la Amada tocada ya
    de cardenillo, roya
    negra, verdín más
    oscuro. Horas
    previstas vueltas
    insomnio reordenando
    el tiempo en una
    dimensión espectral
    donde el quehacer es
    efigie de piedra, piedra
    molecular (secular):
    dadle la vuelta al reloj
    de arena (el espejo)
    y veréis números
    revueltos (espejismos)
    de aserrín. Nada en
    particular me consterna,
    nada lo detiene en sus
    revoluciones, no sé
    qué es agua o qué es
    madera, dónde estoy,
    quién me anima o
    ejecuta (¿cambiará
    pronto mi nombre?).
    Me visto, es de
    mañana, a primera
    hora por el reloj de
    sol, una hora indistinta
    en el reloj de pared,
    mecánico y ulterior.
    Paso al cuarto de
    baño, me sumerjo

disintegration.
Of the guiding star, of the wrinkled hand that gives shelter, the
tender momentary glance
in the glimmering
eyes of the Beloved
brushed already by
verdigris, black rust,
darkest moss. Hours
seen before come back
insomnia rearranging
time into a ghostly
dimension where the
daily task is an effigy
of stone, molecular
(secular) stone:
turn the hourglass
(the mirror)
upside down
and you'll see
scrambled numbers
(mirages) of
sawdust. Nothing
in particular disturbs
me, nothing stops time
in its revolutions, I
don't know what's water,
what's wood, where I
am, who encourages
or executes me (will
my name change at any
moment?). I get dressed,
it's morning, first hour
by the sun dial, an
unreadable hour on
the wall clock, that
mechanical
latecomer. I step

en el espejo del
botiquín (solipsismo
del azogue) detrás
oigo cascos sacar
brillo al asfalto, a
la última piedra,
me implican las
alas extendidas
de extremo a
extremo del
querubín, en el
atrio, dentro del
templo, a la puerta
del Paraíso me voy
prosternando, y al
bajar la vista oigo
(las nueve en punto
de la

mañana)
el
campanillazo.

into the bathroom,
immerse myself in
the medicine cabinet
mirror (mercury's
solipsism) at its back
I hear hoof beats
set the asphalt
shining, from the
last stone, I am
caught in the
cherub's wings
stretched wide from tip
to tip, in the atrium,
inside the temple, at
the gates of Paradise
I'm there bowing
low, and as I
lower my gaze I hear
(exactly nine
in the

morning)
the
deafening
bell.

Véase, como dice Eduardo Espina, que todo es mental

Voy alargando el amanecer, ese continente:
        amanece sideral, con
        el doble de planetas
        en nuestro sistema
        solar, les pongo
        nombre, y no por
        duplicado a los
        planetas nuevos,
        están habitados:
        prolongo la ablución
        con agua tibia, jabón
        de glicerina aroma a
        lavanda, a aceite de
        oliva, me enjuago,
        me cepillo la prótesis
        diente a diente, hago
        gárgaras con agua
        oxigenada (nada más
        barato): y limpio los
        intersticios con hilo
        dental y detrás. Un
        mondadientes de
        cerdas finas para
        mis apretujados
        dientes de hurí,
        evito por todos los
        medios posibles
        caspa y sarro. Diez,
        quince minutos en
        que no tengo sombra,
        no hay pensamiento,
        siento el acto de la
        limpieza como si me
        adentrara en una
        morada más interior,
        una de aquéllas que

Wherein it is seen how, as Eduardo Espina says, it's all in the mind

Gradually I'm stretching out dawn, that continent:
  star-filled
  dawn, with twice
  the planets of our
  solar system, I name
  them, and so the new
  planets won't be
  duplicates, they're
  inhabited: I prolong
  my ablutions with
  warm water, soap
  made of lavender-
  and-olive-oil-
  scented glycerin, I
  rinse, brush my
  dentures one tooth at
  a time, gargle
  with hydrogen
  peroxide (nothing
  cheaper): and I clean
  the gaps and behind
  the teeth with dental
  floss. A toothpick with
  fine bristles for my
  tightly squeezed
  houri's teeth,
  I avoid by all possible
  means dandruff and
  tartar. Ten, fifteen
  minutes where I'm
  without shadow, with no
  thought, I feel
  the act of cleaning
  as if I were going
  deeper and deeper into

elaborara Santa
Teresa en su visión,
vaya coco el mío.

Petronila, ayuda acá a tender la colombina
de hierro en la que
quepo ajustado
cual féretro.

Vamos a sentarnos a la mesa en parejas a
mirar salir de las
tahonas el pan
de flauta.

El pan no llega así como así a la mesa: ven,
Petronila, esto cuaja
despacio. En el
laberinto de la
semilla tiene que
prender hacia
afuera lo que
está debajo: la
espiga, encañar.
Fíjate qué lenta
hormiga el grano
madurar. Siégalo,
tríllalo, aviéntalo,
déjalo reposar
(barbechar)
muélelo, pásalo
por el cedazo,
ayuda acá a
cargar los sacos
de yute a reventar
cuando ha llovido
bien en los campos.

the most inward
dwelling place,
one of those Saint
Teresa might create in her
vision, my mind's power
amazes me.

Petronila, help here to stretch out the iron folding
bed where I
squeeze in tight
as in a coffin.

Let's go and sit at the table in couples and watch the long
crusty loaves
come out of the
baker's oven.

The bread doesn't just appear on the table straight away: come,
Petronila, let it
settle slowly. In
the seed's labyrinth
what's inside
must blaze
outwards: the
ear of wheat must
take hold. Watch
how like a patient
ant the grain
ripens. Reap it,
thresh it, fan it,
let it rest (leave
fallow) grind it,
sift it, now help load
the jute sacks to
bursting when the
rain's been good
in the fields.

El pan está limpio, las manos llagadas: todos
    conformes, salud del
    Orbe, y el día apenas
    comienza.

Amiga, digerir tiene lo suyo, que del gaznate
    al esfínter el trecho
    es largo y animal. A
    resultas de lo cual,
    con un poco de
    esfuerzo podría
    detener el tiempo
    largo y mineral,
    sostenerme
    separado: y
    mientras Dios
    hace de las
    suyas, y por ahí
    se afanan en los
    actos de destrucción,
    ando yo caliente, de
    hombros encogidos,
    subrepticio en mi
    dormitorio, todavía
    en pijama (listado)
    no será de seda
    pero tampoco soy
    la mona que se
    queda.

El único reloj en casa, de flora. Equidistante
    del reloj de sol en
    la plaza. Las tres
    de la tarde no
    son siquiera las
    ocho de la mañana.
    Una caravana. La

The bread is fresh, our hands sore: everyone's happy,
    good health to the
    globe, and the day
    scarcely begun.

My friend, digestion has its own system, from throat to
    sphincter the
    distance is long and
    all animal instinct. And
    consequently, with a
    little effort I could
    stop the long stretch of
    mineral time, could
    keep myself
    apart: and while
    God does his own
    thing, and the world more
    or less competes in
    acts of destruction,
    what do I care,
    with a shrug of my
    shoulders, hiding in
    my bedroom, still
    in (striped) pajamas
    they mightn't be a silk
    purse but I'm still no
    sow's ear.

The only clock in the house, a flower
    clock. Equidistant
    from the sundial in
    the square. Three
    in the afternoon
    it isn't, any
    more than
    eight in the morning.
    A desert caravan.

guía, Petronila,
dirige mi mirada
del borde de la
colombina al
cuaderno de
apuntes (hora)
al libro abierto
sobre el escritorio
(hora) a la
muchedumbre
iluminada (hora
de los bodhisatvas):
insectos agolpándose
allá afuera, contra
la ventana el árbol
centenario de la
acera. Aquí podría
extenderme un poco
más, corretear,
entretejer, ponerme
a vislumbrar acechos
y destellos entre las
sombras, pero ya
(mental) sería vicio.

The guide,
Petronila, directs my
gaze from the edge of
the folding bed to the
sketchbook (one hour)
to the open book on
the writing desk (another
hour) to the
enlightened
horde (hour of
the bodhisattvas):
insects thronging
there outside, the
hundred-year-old
tree on the sidewalk
leaning against the
window. Here I
could wax a little more
expansive, rush
about, make connections,
start to spot places of
ambush and sparks
in the shadows, but
maybe that's now
a bad (mental) habit.

Véase como reencarnar no vale la pena

En la escarpia de la sala cuelga mi madre,
        quiero decir, su último
        vestido del que soy su
        andrajo, caso de volver
        a nacer.

Nacer de la seroja, y reconocer años después
        (acto primero de la
        conciencia) que no
        siento el menor
        atractivo por la
        existencia.

La hierba cana crece entre las entrañas de mi
        madre, lleva una eternidad
        pariendo, sólo cuando
        descansa descuelga de
        la escarpia el vestido a
        rayas, fondo amarillo,
        le llega al tobillo, se
        deshace el dobladillo,
        ahora se tiene que
        sentar otra vez a
        rehacerlo.

Llegan los primeros rascones de la temporada,
        se posan entre la hierba,
        vienen cargados del
        propio reflejo (aterido)
        que han recogido de
        la superficie de los ríos:
        su canto se considera
        desagradable, yo lo
        venero del mismo modo

Wherein it is seen how reincarnation isn't worth the trouble

On the hook in the lounge room hangs my mother, I mean
    her last dress, of
    which I am the
    rags, in case I am
    reborn.

To be born from leaf mulch, and realize years later (first
    act of awareness)
    I don't feel the
    least attraction to
    existence.

Groundsel grows in the entrails of my mother, she takes
    an eternity giving
    birth, only when
    she rests does she
    pick up off the hook the
    striped dress with yellow
    background, it reaches
    her ankles, the hem comes
    undone, now she's
    got to sit down
    again to redo it.

The first rails of the season arrive, land in the tall grass, they bring
    with them their own
    (frozen) reflection skimmed
    off the surface of rivers: their
    song is considered
    unpleasant, I revere it just as
    I don't revere having been
    reborn, in case it
    happens or has happened:
    nor should my mother have

que no venero haber
vuelto a nacer, caso
de que así sea o haya
sido: ni mi madre tener
que padecer de nuevo
la ignominia doble de
la penetración y del
parto. Vinaza espesa
el semen último de mi
padre, la fuente huele
a purín a la hora del
parto, y yo, una vez
más, me veo sometido
a la contrariedad de
una existencia entre
rascones, maloja,
totíes, jardines
invadidos de
pamplinas: enfermizo,
receloso, todo me
intimida con relativa
facilidad.

Cuesta
arriba,
cada
vez
más
empinada,
en
la
cima
otra
vez
tener
que
trepar,

to suffer again the double
shame of penetration and
child birth. The thick dregs
of my father's last semen, the
fountain smells like
liquid manure at the hour
of birth, and I see myself,
once more, submitted to
the contrariness of an
existence among rails,
corn fodder, blackbirds,
gardens invaded by
chickweed: sickly,
suspicious, everything
intimidates me relatively
easily.

Up
hill,
at
each
moment
the
slope
steeper
and
steeper,
at
the
peak
having
to
climb
again,
the
steps
narrow,

se
estrechan
los
escalones,
falta
aire,
sobra
distancia,
cómo
llegar
a la mesa del desayuno desde allá arriba, eso
     es tarea de jayanes. Y
     todo por una colación
     de gañanes, un cacho
     turbio de pan con serrín,
     brebaje insípido de
     aroma dudoso, y tener
     luego que volver a
     rastrillar, sembrar
     filones de materia
     muerta entre pesos
     amañados desde lo
     alto, medidas que
     son ficción del número.
     Y el vestido final, ése,
     sigue ahí, a la entrada,
     en la sala, motas,
     borras, polvillo de
     mariposas, polen
     descompuesto. Lo
     voy a descolgar,
     ponérmelo, quitar la
     sábana del espejo
     de cuerpo entero a
     mano derecha,
     mirarme por delante
     ante el espejo a

short
of
breath,
more
distance
to
go,
how
to
reach
the breakfast table from up there, a job strictly for the
      tough guys. And all
      for a farmhands'
      snack, a muddied hunk of
      bread with sawdust, an
      insipid bowl of dubious
      fragrance, and then
      back to raking, sowing
      veins of dead matter
      according to weights
      rigged from above, the
      measurements all a
      numerical fiction. And
      the final dress, that one,
      still there, at the entrance,
      in the living room, specks
      of dust, fluff, powder from
      moths, decomposed pollen.
      I'm going to take it
      down, put it on, remove the
      sheet from the full-length
      mirror to the right, look at
      myself in front of the
      mirror knowing full well
      behind me and
      before me I see nothing.

sabiendas que no
veo detrás ni delante,
nada.

Seroja,
pamplinas,
y
en
la
escarpia,
una
de
dos:
ella
o
yo.
El
guiñapo
(yo)
o
el
pingajo
embebido
en
una
sangre
menstrual.

Leaf
mulch,
chickweed,
and
on
the
hook,
one
or
the
other,
a
choice:
she
or
me.
The
ragman
(me)
or
the
small
rag
soaked
in
menstrual
blood.

Devastación

Nadie se mueva, Dios entró en acción, la
    avena loca invade, la
    langosta (faraónica)
    llevando la carcoma
    a cuestas, arrasa:
    morir, morir, qué alivio,
    dejar de renquear,
    sentir la falta de aire,
    de apetito, dejar de
    ser el tullido de la casa,
    a la mañana sangrar
    las almorranas, a
    menos que luego haya
    otra vida, y en la otra
    almorranas, baldaduras,
    halitosis, sobaquina y
    la madre que nos parió
    sigan haciendo de las
    suyas: cuerpo a la
    muerte enganchado
    para siempre. No se
    mueva nadie que me
    voy a poner a bailar
    entre langostas, a la
    solapa del saco avena
    loca, carcoma a la boca:
    bailar del brazo de Osip
    Mandelstam, Nikolay
    Gumilyov, Bely, Blok,
    en Slepnyovo, Tsarskoye
    Selo, Ajmatova, trompetillas
    a Lenin, pedos en la cara a
    Stalin para que huela a sus
    muertos. Nadie se mueva
    que el día es irreversible,

Devastation

Don't anybody move, God's leapt into action, wild seeds
    invade, (pharaonic)
    locusts carrying woodworm
    on their bodies, lay waste:
    to die, to die, what a relief,
    no more limping along, feeling
    the loss of breath, loss of
    appetite, at last to stop being
    the household cripple,
    hemorrhoids bleeding in
    the morning, unless
    there's another life, and in
    that life hemorrhoids,
    crippling diseases, halitosis,
    underarm odor and mother
    who gave birth to us
    let them go on ruling the
    roost: our body
    forever hooked on
    death. Don't anybody
    move, I'm going to start
    dancing among locusts,
    on my jacket's lapel
    wild seeds, woodworm
    on my lips: to dance
    arm in arm with Osip
    Mandelstam, Nikolay
    Gumilyov, Bely, Blok,
    in Slepnyovo, Tsarkoye
    Selo, with Akhmatova,
    blowing raspberries at
    Lenin, farting in Stalin's
    face so he can smell
    his own dead. Don't anybody
    move, the day is

se sale de los cuadrantes,
la hora rompe la esfera, en
las astillas del número, ora
arábigo, ora romano, Dios
dirige el cotarro: los ruidos
son pocos, pies danzantes
de aire baten estepas de
aire carentes de distancia,
de paso, de exoneración.
Un ruido de mandíbulas,
de avena loca invadiendo
los graneros del Faraón,
graneros del Zar, el ruido de
la carcoma en las espigas,
en la médula de la madera
de los juegos de silla y mesa
del comedor, en los tronos
de algún que otro nuevo
potentado escondiéndose
de Dios. Fuera, y en fila
india todos, seguid al
guión, ave vieja que todo
lo sabe, conoce las rutas
perpendiculares, la diagonal,
el diámetro sin destino, la
vertical final, cuando asesta.
Reíd. Todo a la muerte. Tres
o cuatro poetas rusos que
todo lo vieron, unas pocas
langostas ahítas de avena
loca, la boca y ano cubiertos
de carcoma. El último ruido,
un poco de serrín, contrapaso,
y en representación quiebro
el pie, trenzo el paso, no se
mueve del terebinto una
hoja, del omaso de la

irreversible, it's right
off the grid, the hour
shatters the sphere, into
splinters of the number,
now Arabic, now Roman,
God directs the rabble: not
much sound, dancing feet
of air beat against the windy
steppes devoid of distance,
step-less, no way through, no
exoneration. Noise of jaws
grinding, of wild seeds invading
Pharaoh's granaries, the Tsar's
granaries, gnawing sound of
woodworm in the wheat
sprigs, in the wooden pith
that forms the core of a set
of chairs round the dining
room table, in the thrones of
some new potentate or other
hiding from God. Out front,
and all in Indian file, follow
the guide, the old bird who
knows everything, knows the
perpendicular paths, the
diagonal way, the diameter
with no future, the vertical
plummet of the final smash.
Laugh. Everything rushing
to death. Three or four
Russian poets who saw it
all, a few locusts glutted
with wild seeds, their mouth
and anus covered in
woodworm. The last
sound, a little sawdust, a
contrapaso, in performance

vaca roja exuda caseína,
caseína muerta, voz de
hez en las alturas no
llega Dios.

I break my foot, twist my
step, not a leaf stirs on the
terebinth, casein oozes from
the red cow's omasum, dead
casein, the voice of dregs
on the heights no sign
of God.

Dos Índoles, una Devastación

Propercio
aspira
a
Cintia,
a Guadalupe, yo: soy acogido, años de
    recogimiento en su
    regazo, garantía de
    una mano, cierto
    que callosa mas
    acogedora mano,
    a la hora de
    (brasas) (rescoldos
    pulverizados) de la
    Muerte: Propercio,
    opuesto caso, se vio
    siempre repudiado.
    Siendo igual de
    devoto, ¿repudiado?
    ¿A santo de qué?
    Yo, y sé que juego
    con ventaja, entiendo
    el caso: no era aseado
    ni hacendoso, se
    bañaba rara vez,
    halitosis, no se
    limpiaba el fondillo
    tras la deposición, y
    para colmo, la mala
    digestión viciaba la
    habitación de flatos
    irrespirables: ¿qué
    pedirles, Propercio,
    a Doris, a Cornelia?
    ¿A Cintia? Cintia, de
    barqueros manoseada,
    en redondo preñada

Two Indoles, a Devastation

Propertius
yearns
for
Cynthia,
I for Guadalupe: I am under her protection, years of
shelter in her lap, a
hand's pledge,
the certainty
of a life-worn yet
welcoming hand,
at the hour of
(embers) (pulverized
ashes) of
Death: Propertius,
complete opposite, was
constantly repudiated.
With equal devotion,
repudiated? Why
on earth? I, and I know
I've got the edge here,
understand his
situation: he wasn't
one for hygiene or
housework, rarely
bathed, halitosis, he
didn't clean his
backside after bowel
movements, and, to
top it all, poor
digestion filled the
room with unbreathable
farts: Propertius, what
do you expect from them,
Doris, Cornelia? Cynthia?
Cynthia, pawed over by
sailors, impregnated

de cabo a rabo, por
los cuatro costados,
de dentro afuera, por
el efebo de turno,
bucles negros, ojos
zarcos, frente
estrecha, sienes
espesas que (todo
el vecindario lo sabe)
prefiere un barquero,
un centurión, a Cintia.
Guadalupe en cambio
hizo de mí naturaleza,
y yo de Guadalupe,
cáliz. Advocación.
Jocalias. Y mejor,
a primera hora el
café que nos aproxima
entre palabras un
tanto irregulares,
a dejar pasar un
cierto malestar de
época, cubrir de
un tul fácil de rasgar
epitelios, capas,
membranas, arterias
(arteriolas) vasos
deferentes a las
trompas (concavidades)
arrecifes: en un
cuerpo a cuerpo
gestar (hará pronto
cuatro décadas)
perfección (del Reino)
en el reino (malestar
de época) desvencijado.
Ahí

every which way, top to
toe, inside out, by some
ephebe in the queue, black
curls, light-blue eyes, narrow
forehead, greasy temples, who
(the whole neighborhood
knows) prefers a sailor,
a centurion, to Cynthia.
Guadalupe in contrast
has fashioned from my
nature, and I from hers,
a perfect calyx. Avocation.
The altar's sacred vessels.
And better, first thing in
the morning, coffee to bring
us together among somewhat
hit or miss words, not to
mention our decidedly out-
of-joint times, to cover with
an easily torn veil
epithelia, layers,
membranes, arteries
(arterioles) vas
deferens to the
tubes (hollows)
reefs: in body to body
struggle to give birth to
(it will soon be four
decades) perfection
(of the Kingdom) in
this (our out-of-joint
times) dilapidated
kingdom.
There

somos
dos
águilas
defendiéndonos,
dos
linces
de
a
como
sea
la
casa
sosteniendo,
yo
vendo
escombros,
Guadalupe
cuece
pan.
Pudimos
(podremos:
hay
que
confiar).
Esta
tarde compartimos en voz alta unos poemas
    de Propercio, no nos
    atañen lamentaciones
    ni su mal de amores. Su
    aflicción (producto de
    las indignidades de una
    pésima digestión) nos
    hace encogernos de
    hombros. Cintia, una
    ficción; Propercio se
    vaya de putas. A
    nosotros, si algo nos

we
are
two
eagles
defending
ourselves,
two
sharp
eyes
upholding
the
house
from
no
matter
what,
I
sell
rubble,
Guadalupe
bakes
bread.
We
coped
(will
cope:
you've
got
to
trust).
This
afternoon we share aloud some poems by Propertius,
    his lamentations and
    misfortunes in love are
    none of our concern. His
    affliction (a product of very
    bad digestion and its

aflige hoy por hoy es
un asunto de dinero
(pasará) y el otro:
uña que carne
desgarra, mil naves
surtas a la espera,
cuál nos toca que
no hay faros, nadie
escapa, los riscos
de la costa demasiado
altos, última escala
ser embarcados,
pasarela, estruendo,
la barca (pecios,
nosotros) estrellada:
Cintia enterrada en
versos de Propercio,
y yo de

Guadalupe
(candado)
yéndome
por
costaneras
(diente
de
perro)
a
un
confín
cada
vez
más
cercano:
la
silaba
se

indignities) just makes us
shrug our shoulders.
Cynthia, a fiction;
Propertius, let him go visit
a brothel. For us, if
something afflicts us day
by day it's money worries
(they will pass) and the
other matter: a toenail that
tears the flesh, a thousand
ships lie calmly ready, which
one will take us as there's
no lighthouses, the coastal
cliffs too high, the last port
for embarkation, gangway,
a thunder clap, the boat
(we're now flotsam)
shattered: Cynthia buried in
poems of Propertius,
and I in poems of

Guadalupe
(padlocked)
walking
shoreline
paths
(jagged
limestone
outcrops)
to
a
far
edge
that's
always
closer:
the

acaba,
el
ojo
remoto
aguas
ignotas
remonta
(se
desmorona)
y
Guadalupe
(viva
brasa
todavía)
destapa
(tapa)
guarda
(cierra
la

gaveta).

syllable
ends,
the
distant
eye
heads
upstream
on
unknown
waters
(breaks
up)
and
Guadalupe
(a
live
coal
still)
reveals
(conceals)
puts
away
(closes
the
drawer).

De la nación

En mi país no crece el croco, crece
    (con creces) el yeso
    desmoronado.

No pienso revelar el nombre de mi
    país. No tiene sentido
    constatar las cadenas
    de muladares (pudrideros)
    a lo largo del majá que
    es el país: a lo ancho
    del carey que es hoy
    su desierto.

Puedo aludir a sus dos grandes ciudades
    haciendo hincapié en
    la ausencia de cúpulas,
    minaretes, no hay
    casas de techos
    puntiagudos, no
    hay mansardas, no
    quedan asideros: en
    las tazas, el aire, la
    circunferencia de
    los plátanos de
    Indias: notable la
    falta de barandas,
    balaustradas,
    cariátides, náyades,
    las madres que nos
    sostengan (cuartos
    desconchados, los
    salones con sus
    suelos de losa
    picados, manchas
    de humedad donde
    colgaran las arañas).

Of the nation

In my country crocuses don't grow, crumbling plaster
    grows (in
    abundance).

I don't intend to reveal the name of my country. It makes
    no sense to verify the
    long line of (rotting)
    dung heaps down
    the length of the
    harmless boa that
    is my country: wide
    as the turtle shell which
    is nowadays its desert.

I could allude to its two big cities emphasizing the
    absence of cupolas, of
    minarets, there are
    no houses with pointed
    roofs, no attics, there's
    nothing to hold
    onto: on cups, the
    air, the circumference
    of Oriental Plane
    trees: a notable
    absence of
    verandas, balustrades,
    caryatids, naiads,
    mothers who might
    support us (flaking
    bedrooms, living
    rooms with
    cracked stone
    floors, damp
    patches where
    spiders maybe
    hang).

Red de helechos la escayola gris veteada de
        blanco ennegrecido,
        el aire apesta: apesta
        la llama azul de los
        infiernillos y las
        cocinas, ubres de
        hollín.

El campo es hermoso. A la tarde veríamos
        sentadas en sendas
        comadritas (inmóviles)
        en el porche de madera,
        tablones desvencijados,
        la mosca mortificando a
        la araña cansada de
        rehacer la tela, la araña
        hambrienta se apresta
        con las pocas fuerzas
        que le quedan, la
        mosca entrega su
        reflejo, una sombra,
        aplauden (ladeándose,
        se agarran la cabeza)
        Ajmátova y Tsvetaeva.

Éste sería el momento de revelar el nombre,
        dimensiones, datos
        estadísticos, condición
        actual de mi país. Lo
        haría, no con gusto,
        pero lo haría si no
        fuera por la condición
        actual del país.

A una hora de la capital está el cementerio,
        en línea recta al norte
        (a una hora) Caronte:

A network of ferns grey plaster with blackened white
　　veins, the air stinks:
　　the blue flame of spirit
　　stoves and kitchens
　　stinks, udders of
　　soot.

The countryside is beautiful. In the evening we'd see sitting
　　there (motionless) two
　　swing chairs on
　　each wooden
　　porch, rickety
　　planks, the fly teasing
　　the spider who's worn out
　　remaking its web, with
　　what little strength it
　　has left the hungry
　　spider exerts itself, the
　　fly yields its reflection, its
　　shadow, (leaning over,
　　holding onto their
　　heads) Akhmatova and
　　Tsvetayeva applaud.

This would be the moment to reveal the name, dimensions,
　　statistical facts, present
　　condition of my country.
　　I would do so, not
　　enthusiastically, but I
　　would do so if it weren't
　　for the present condition
　　of my country.

One hour from the capital is the cemetery, in a straight
　　line to the north (one
　　hour) Charon: explosions

a izquierda y derecha
las deflagraciones, a
unos pasos a la salida
de casa, nuestros
famosos venados de
piedra caliza: los
chiquillos ven ballenas
blancas, los mayores
la arena negra manifiesta
de los playazos al borde
de la destrucción, y las
gentes que a veces
nos visitan miran el
vuelo desarticulado
de los buitres.

to left and right, a few
steps after leaving
home, our famous
limestone deer: the
little ones see white
whales, the elderly
the black sand that's
evident on long
beaches on the edge
of destruction, and
those who from time to
time visit us watch the
erratic flight of
vultures.

Acta

Para Soleida Ríos

Cuba, candado.

En las puertas de hierro de las ferreterías,
    bien podría llamarlas
    tlapalerías, llamarlas
    escoria, agua vana
    del hierro, daría lo
    mismo.

Cuba, cagafierro.

Candente, ascuas agujereando (¿pero más
    todavía?) los comercios
    de hormigón, cemento
    despintado, surtidores
    de orín: purín. Podría
    llamarlos polvo de
    guano, plasta del
    yarey, de veras
    que a estas alturas,
    brotes a cal y canto
    de plumbago, da lo
    mismo.

Isla por antonomasia confirmada a todo
    lo largo en los
    muladares, los
    humilladeros,
    toba rota a
    Levante, la
    estrechez del
    agua, dónde
    está el centro,
    dónde está el

Acta

For Soleida Ríos

Cuba, padlocks.

On the iron doors of hardware shops, you could
    of course call them
    ironmongers, call them
    slag, useless liquid
    iron, it's all
    one.

Cuba, iron dross.

Red hot, embers burning holes (still now?) in stores
    made of concrete,
    the cement's paint
    worn off, fountains
    of rust, liquid
    manure. I could
    call it guano
    dust, palm leaf
    dung, at these
    heights, the plumbago's
    tight-locked shoots,
    truly it's all the
    same.

Quintessential island confirmed its entire length
    in dung
    heaps, paupers'
    graves, broken
    tuff to the East, a
    narrow strait of
    water, where's
    the center,
    where's the

centro, las
canteras a
Poniente,
desmoronadas.

Se fue el caimán, se fueron los quedados,
    nos fuimos todos,
    se nos reconoce
    por la tira de
    maloja anudada
    al ojal del saco.

Una bibijagua roja, marca de la candela,
    viene a allanar,
    se va a comer el
    ojal, tráncala que
    nos vamos.

La bijirita, brasa que se iba a posar, zunzún
    agitado ante la corola
    abierta de par en par
    del hibisco, se va
    extenuando boca
    de fuego al suelo.

Eran los últimos trámites, por qué puerta,
    cuáles rejas, qué
    trancas oxidadas,
    vamos por pasos:
    lo primero cerrar
    los espejos, vaciar
    la luz de sus motas,
    el trapo de sus
    borras, polvo de
    yute a la boca:
    traga, ciudadano,
    cabilla, al final
    sentarnos en

center, to
the West
stone quarries,
crumbling away.

The caiman has gone, those left have gone,
we've all gone, you
can recognize us from
the twist of corn stalk
knotted into the
buttonhole of a
jacket.

A red leafcutter ant, a stamp of fire, comes
to raze the ground,
goes off to eat the
buttonhole, lock it
up as we leave.

The flame-throated warbler, an ember about to land, an excited
hummingbird above
the hibiscus' wide
open corolla, vanishes
exhausted its blazing
barrel in the dust.

The last questions of red tape, through what door, which grilles,
what rusted iron
bars, let's go
step by step: first
to fold away the
mirrors, empty the light
of dust motes, the
cleaning rag of fluff, lift
jute shavings to your lips:
down the hatch, citizen,
the iron rod, in the end
for us to sit down as

familia, sillones
de cuje, garabatos,
hebras sueltas de
tabaco, limpiarse
las comisuras y
ponerse a narrar.

De la partida, del tumulto de los bicharracos
tapiando sobre
tapiado para
acabar de
cerrar: candado
doble, colibrí
comido a medias,
está de fiesta la
bibijagua, se vació
el vacío: échale
tierra, échale
mofuco que son
las tres de la tarde,
todo líquido, y arde
de punta a punta.

a family, easy chairs made
from rough vines, all
squiggly, loose threads
of tobacco, to lick the
corners of your mouth
clean and start telling
stories.

Of leaving, of the din of burrowing insects piling walls
on top of walls to
close finally for
good: double
locks, half-eaten
hummingbird, the
leafcutter ant's
delighted, emptiness
has been emptied:
bury it, drown it
in three o'clock in
the afternoon moonshine,
pure liquid, and it burns
end to end.